CAMBRIDGE

EMPOWER

PRE-INTERMEDIATE
ACADEMIC SKILLS
AND READING PLUS

B1

Adrian Doff, Craig Thaine, David Rea

CAMBRIDGE
UNIVERSITY PRESS

University Printing House, Cambridge CB2 8BS, United Kingdom

One Liberty Plaza, 20th Floor, New York, NY 10006, USA

477 Williamstown Road, Port Melbourne, VIC 3207, Australia

314–321, 3rd Floor, Plot 3, Splendor Forum, Jasola District Centre, New Delhi – 110025, India

79 Anson Road, #06–04/06, Singapore 079906

Cambridge University Press is part of the University of Cambridge.

It furthers the University's mission by disseminating knowledge in the pursuit of education, learning and research at the highest international levels of excellence.

www.cambridge.org
Information on this title: www.cambridge.org/978-1-108-719049

First published 2019

20 19 18 17 16 15 14 13 12 11 10 9 8 7 6 5 4 3 2 1

Printed in the United Kingdom by Latimer Trend

A catalogue record for this publication is available from the British Library

ISBN 978-1-107-46651-7 Pre-intermediate Student's Book
ISBN 978-1-107-46652-4 Pre-intermediate Student's Book with Online Assessment
    and Practice, and Online Workbook
ISBN 978-1-107-46666-1 Pre-intermediate Student's Interactive eBook
ISBN 978-1-107-46667-8 Pre-intermediate Student's Interactive eBook
    with Online Assessment and Practice, and Online Workbook
ISBN 978-1-107-46671-5 Pre-intermediate Teacher's Book
ISBN 978-1-107-46655-5 Pre-intermediate Class Audio CDs (3)
ISBN 978-1-107-46665-4 Pre-intermediate Class DVD
ISBN 978-1-107-46668-5 Pre-intermediate Presentation Plus DVD-ROM
ISBN 978-1-107-46680-7 Pre-intermediate Workbook with Answers, with downloadable Audio
ISBN 978-1-107-48876-2 Pre-intermediate Workbook without Answers, with downloadable Audio

Additional resources for this publication at www.cambridge.org/empower

To students and teachers

Academic Skills Plus

The first part of this books gives you practice of academic skills and language:

- an extra lesson for every Student's Book unit, linked by topic
- practise all four skills: listening, speaking, reading and writing
- includes language and study skills for academic purposes
- helps develop critical thinking skills
- texts and audio recordings reflect real-life academic studies

Students: You can download the audio files from e-Source, using the access code in the cover of this book. Please go to: https://esource.cambridge.org

Teachers: The audio files are available in the Cambridge Learning Management System (CLMS) in the Teacher's Resources section. Please go to: https://www.cambridgelms.org. Also available on the Empower website (please go to: cambridge.org/empower).

Full teacher's notes, with additional tips and ideas, are also available as free downloadable PDFs in the CLMS or on the Empower website.

Reading Plus

The second part of this book provides extra reading lessons to complement the Student's Book:

- an additional Reading lesson for every Student's Book unit, linked by topic
- longer and more challenging reading texts, with activities, to use in class or at home
- strategies to improve reading skills in the *Better Reading* box

Teachers:

Full teacher's notes, with additional tips and ideas, are available as free photocopiable PDFs in the CLMS in the Teacher's Resources section. Please go to: https://www.cambridgelms.org. Also available on the Empower website (cambridge.org/empower).

Also available for students using the Student's Book with Online Assessment and Practice:

Academic Skills Online Practice

Extra practice of academic listening and reading skills on the Cambridge Learning Management System (CLMS):

- complements and extends the Academic Skills Plus lessons in this book
- academic listening and reading skills, plus a focus on key language
- suitable for self-study
- scores appear in the CLMS gradebook

Where to find the Online Practice:

Use the code in the Student's Book to access the CLMS. Then go to the Academic Skills tab.

Contents

Academic Skills Plus

Unit and topic	Listening and Speaking	Reading and Writing	Critical Thinking	Language Focus
Unit 1 Communication				
Communication studies: Linguistics	**L** Outlining the content of a presentation **S** Saying what you are going to talk about		Thinking about aims	Saying what you are going to talk about
Unit 2 Global tourism				
Business studies: Tourism management		**R** Understanding statistics; Scanning for facts and figures **W** Describing changes and trends; Writing based on visual information	Thinking about the ideas in a text	Describing changes and trends
Unit 3 Spending money				
Economics: How people spend money	**L** Noticing lecture structure; Listening for key points **S** Discourse markers to show contrast		Applying new knowledge	Language of contrast
Unit 4 Social rituals				
Sociology: Selfies	**L** Main points and details **S** Defining new words and terms in a presentation		Using mind maps to summarise information	Defining expressions
Unit 5 Study and work				
Economics/Education: Students' part-time work		**R** Reading for main and supporting ideas; Guided notetaking **W** Topic sentences	Recognising and collecting information	Topic sentences
Unit 6 Phobias				
Psychology: Fear	**L** Identifying points from a discussion; Identifying turn-taking strategies **S** Turn-taking in a discussion		Exploring causes and reasons	Sharing ideas – taking turns
Unit 7 Computer games				
Sociology: Technology and children's play		**R** Distinguishing main points and supporting detail; Identifying cohesion / reference markers **W** Adding description / explanation to main ideas; Using substitution and reference for cohesion	Going beyond the text	Referencing with *this* and *these*
Unit 8 Selling music				
Music studies: How music is distributed	**L** Listening to check predictions; Identifying unclear points **S** Checking and clarifying		Matching what you hear with your own opinion	Clarifying and asking questions
Unit 9 Bilingualism				
Applied linguistics: Bilingual education	**L** Listening for main and supporting ideas **S** Making main points		Distinguishing between different kinds of information	Making main points
Unit 10 Shopping				
Business studies: Self-service retail		**R** Identifying evidence to support main points **W** Reporting on facts and opinions	Predicting problems	Reporting facts and opinions
Unit 11 Coffee				
Biology/Environmental studies: Recycling coffee grounds	**L** Listening for main ideas and details; Recognising problem-solution patterns **S** Providing supporting detail in presentations		Analysing patterns / problem-solution	Adding information
Unit 12 Leaving home				
Sociology: Cultural studies		**R** Understanding factual detail **W** Reporting statistical data; Writing from notes	Going beyond the facts	Proportions

Reading Plus

Unit 1 Communication

1 SPEAKING

a 💬 Look at the photos and answer the questions.

1 What topics do you think the people in photos a and b are talking about?
2 What topics do you think the people in photos c and d are talking about?

b 💬 Think about the way men or boys talk together and women or girls talk together. Do you think there are any differences? Talk about:

- topics
- reasons for talking together
- body language (gestures, eye contact, distance)
- how they speak and how they listen
- vocabulary and expressions

2 LISTENING

a 🧠 **CRITICAL THINKING**
THINKING ABOUT AIMS

In your studies, you may have to give presentations to other students. Discuss these questions.

1 What is a presentation?
2 How many parts should there be in a presentation?
3 You usually start a presentation with an introduction. What is the aim of this?

b ▶1.1 You will hear three students giving an introduction to a presentation. Which of these topics is each student going to talk about? Write A (Alex), J (Julie), L (Laura) or N (nobody).

1 how people talk to each other at work ____
2 how boys and girls talk ____
3 how older people and younger people talk ____
4 differences in the way men and women talk ____

c ▶1.1 Listen again to Alex and Julie and complete their notes with words from the box.

examples	features	gender	men
status	women	workplace	

Alex

Communication: differences between _____ and

_____

1 research – general features
2 _____: typical ways men and women
   communicate
3 language _____ – grammar

Julie

Role relationships in the _____ – effect on
communication

1 higher – lower _____ – boss/employee
2 equal status – colleagues
3 _____ – male colleagues, female colleagues

d ▶1.1 Listen again to Laura.

1 How is her introduction different from the others? Do you think this is a good way to start a presentation? Why / Why not?

2 What ideas do the listeners suggest for … ?
   a boys' topics   b girls' topics

3 What does Deborah Tannen's research show about boys and girls? Choose the correct answer (a, b or c).
   a They talk about different topics but use similar language.
   b They talk about similar topics but use different language.
   c They talk about different topics and use different language.

STUDY SKILLS: STARTING A PRESENTATION

Speakers often use a 'hook' – something interesting to get their audience's attention at the start. Think of some different ways to do this and make a list of ideas.

3 PRONUNCIATION *d* and *t* sounds

a ▶1.2 Listen to the sentences below (1–3). What do you notice about the underlined words? Answer the questions.

- are they … ?
  a clearly separated?   b joined together?
- what happens to the *d* or *t* sound?

1 How do men and women communicate and is there a difference?
2 I'm going to describe research that people have done in this area.
3 … people of equal status, so colleagues at work for example.

b Read the sentences. How do you think the underlined words are pronounced? Try saying them to yourself.

1 … we're going to look at three different aspects of this.
2 And the third area is different genders.
3 … in the other part there's a group of girls.
4 … hair and make-up or … which boys they like … yeah.

c ▶1.3 Listen and check. Were they the same as you expected?

4 LANGUAGE FOCUS
Saying what you are going to talk about

a The three speakers started by saying what they are going to talk about. What do you think they said? Add one word to each gap.

1 **Alex:** I'm _____ to describe research that people have done in this area.
2 **Julie:** My talk is _____ role relationships in the workplace.
3 **Laura:** I _____ to talk about her research and I'm going to show you some examples.
4 **Alex:** Then I'd _____ to show you some examples of … typical ways men and women communicate.

b ▶1.4 Listen and check. Which three phrases have a similar meaning?

c ▶1.5 Alex and Julie used the phrases in the box to show the order of topics. Listen and put the phrases in order (1–7) as you hear them.

and lastly _____	then _____	the first one is _____
first of all _____	at the end _____	
the third area is _____	secondly _____	

d If you introduce three topics to talk about, which phrases in 4c can you use … ?

1 for the first topic   3 for the third topic
2 for the second topic   4 for a final discussion

e Complete the gaps in the introduction below. Use expressions from 4a and 4c.

> My talk is ¹_____ communication and I'm ²_____ talk about the difference between the way older and younger people communicate. First of all we're going to look at the way older people speak. ³_____ I'd ⁴_____ look at the way younger people speak and we're ⁵_____ see some examples. And ⁶_____ I want to talk about communication problems between older and younger people. And at ⁷_____ we're going to have a discussion and you can ask questions.

f 💬 Practise giving the introduction in 4e.

1 Look at the notes below and think about phrases you will use.
2 Cover 4e. Give the introduction using only the notes below.

> **Communication: differences between older and younger people**
>
> 1 the way older people speak – examples
> 2 the way younger people speak – examples
> 3 problems of communication (old and young people)
> 4 discussion and questions

5 SPEAKING

a Plan a presentation on one of these topics (or choose a topic of your own).

- communicating with very old people
- English words used in your language
- learning English grammar
- opportunities to listen to English

Make notes like the ones in 4f.

b Prepare your introduction, explaining what you will talk about. Use expressions from 4a and 4c.

c 💬 Work in pairs and take turns to present your topic.

1 Give the introduction to your talk.
2 Listen to your partner's introduction. Was it clear? Did he/she use expressions from 4a and 4c?

Unit 2   Global tourism

ACADEMIC SKILLS PLUS

Business studies: Tourism management

Reading skills: Understanding statistical information; Scanning for facts and figures
Writing skills: Describing changes and trends; Writing a paragraph based on visual information

1 SPEAKING

a 💬 Look at the photos. Which place would you prefer to visit as a tourist? Why?

b 💬 Think about your own country.
1 What countries do tourists come from?
2 What tourist destinations do people from your country go to?
3 How has this changed over the last few years? Think about:
  • numbers of tourists
  • different nationalities
  • new places

c Cover the text. Can you guess the missing information in these statements?
1 In 2013 ____ of the world's population were over 60.
  a 5%   b 12%   c 25%
2 By 2025, about ____ of all tourists will be under 40.
  a 25%   b 50%   c 80%
3 More than ____ people travel as tourists every year.
  a a thousand   b a million   c a billion
4 There were ____ more tourists last year than the year before.
  a 300,000   b 300 million c 300 billion
5 The 'millennial generation' are people who were born after ____.
  a 1980   b 2000   c 2010
6 The middle class is growing in ____.
  a Europe   b Asia   c both Europe and Asia

2 READING

The growth in global tourism

Global tourism is growing very fast and for many countries in the world it is one of the main factors in economic development. With well over a billion tourists a year, 10% of the world's economy comes from tourism. And there has been a steady increase year by year: last year 300 million more tourists travelled the world than in the year before. Tourism provides extra jobs and it helps to improve the balance of the economy in countries which tourists visit because it offers an alternative to more traditional industries. It also brings other benefits, such as cultural exchange and opportunities for language learning.

There's no doubt that tourism is becoming more important. So how is global tourism changing and what will happen in the future? There are four main trends which we believe will influence tourism development.

1 **Silver-haired tourists**. The global population is getting older so there's an important new tourist segment: the over-60s, often known as 'silver-haired tourists'. They are now one of the fastest growing segments of the tourist market. The share of the world's population over the age of 60 has increased from 8% in 1950 to 12% in 2013, and it may grow to 21% by 2050. Older people often have more money to spend and the time to spend it, often because they were in high-paying jobs and are now retired.

2 **The millennial generation**. Millennials, the generation born in the 1980s and 1990s, are also an important market segment, and it is steadily increasing. By 2025, 50% of all tourists will probably be millennials or their children. They have more access to online information than older tourists and they are more likely to use technology when they make choices about their holidays.

3 **The Asian middle class**. Traditionally, travel and tourism was an occupation for people with money, but levels of poverty have decreased and there is a growing global middle class. The middle class will probably increase from 1.8 billion in 2009 to 3.2 billion by 2020 and 4.9 billion by 2030. The majority of the global middle class will come from the Asia-Pacific region and by 2030 they will represent two thirds of the global middle class population. By contrast, the middle class in Europe and North America has stopped growing and so will gradually become a smaller proportion.

a Skills focus Looking for facts and figures

Read the text on page 8 and check your answers to the questions in 1c. Do this as quickly as possible. What was the quickest way to find the answers?

1 finding the numbers and then reading to check
2 reading carefully line by line from the beginning

b Look at the visual information in Figure 1 and Figure 2.

1 Find <u>four</u> sentences in the text which give the same information.
2 Use Figures 1 and 2 to answer these questions.
   a Last year, approximately what percentage of tourists were over 60?
   b How many people in the world were middle class in 2015?

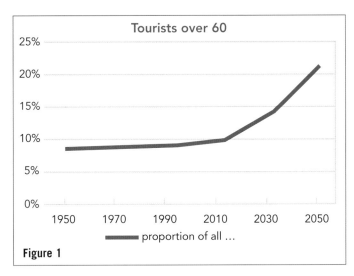

Figure 1

Figure 2

STUDY SKILLS: READING GRAPHS AND CHARTS

1 Which visual is a bar chart and which is a graph?
2 Which is better for showing quantity? Which is better for showing change?

c Which of these things does the text say about global tourism? Answer *Y* (Yes) or *N* (No).

1 Tourism provides new kinds of work for people. _____
2 It is difficult for industrial countries to develop tourism. _____
3 Tourism is an opportunity for people from different countries to meet. _____
4 Older tourists are important because they often spend more money. _____
5 Younger people usually know a lot about the countries they visit. _____
6 In the future, there will be more tourists from Asian countries. _____

d CRITICAL THINKING
THINKING ABOUT THE IDEAS IN A TEXT

1 Why do you think tourism is growing so quickly in the world?
2 The text says 'global tourism' is increasing. Do you think this includes all countries or only some? Why?
3 The article describes positive effects of tourism. What negative effects are there?

3 LANGUAGE FOCUS
Describing changes and trends

a Look at these examples from the text.

1 The middle class **will probably increase** from 1.8 billion in 2009 to 3.2 billion by 2020.
2 The middle class in Europe and North America **has stopped** growing.
3 Global tourism **is growing** very fast.
4 It **may grow** to 21% by 2050.

Which sentences are about … ?

a a change from the past to now _____
b a change going on at the moment _____
c a possible change in the future _____ _____

Match the examples to the verb forms.

a modal verb (x2) _____ _____
b present continuous _____
c present perfect simple _____

b Look at these examples and answer the questions below.

1 The cost of air travel has **decreased**.
2 There has been a steady **increase** in global tourism year by year.
3 Millennials are an important market segment and it is steadily **increasing**.
4 There has been a **decrease** in the levels of poverty.

a Which words in **bold** mean 'more'? Which mean 'less'?
b Which are verbs and which are nouns? After the nouns, what word comes next?
c Which syllable is stressed in each word?

c Complete the gaps with words in the box (you may need to change the form of the word). You will need to use one word twice.

increase	decrease	change	become

1 Because of fears about safety, there has been a _____ in tourism to North Africa.
2 There's no doubt that millennial tourists are _____ more important.
3 The number of Asian tourists in Europe has _____ over the last 10 years because of the growing middle class.
4 Because of the internet, the cost of accommodation has generally _____ and you can now stay cheaply in most cities.
5 It isn't certain how global tourism will _____ in the future and whether the present trend will continue.

4 WRITING

a Look at the graph and discuss the questions.

1 What are the different coloured lines? What are the numbers along the bottom of the graph? What are the numbers on the right?
2 Does the graph tell us about … ?
   a tourism inside a country
   b tourists visiting other countries
3 What does the graph tell us about Chinese tourists?

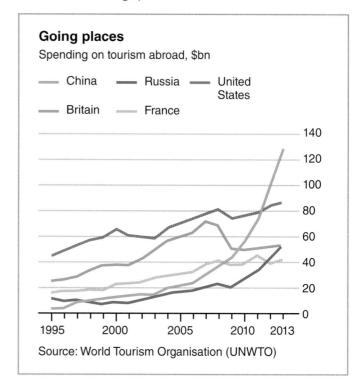

Going places
Spending on tourism abroad, $bn

— China — Russia ···· United States
— Britain ···· France

Source: World Tourism Organisation (UNWTO)

b Read these notes about Chinese tourism. What do you think the text will say?

The growth of Chinese tourism

rapid increase – Chinese tourists

1 in 10 tourists – Chinese

more money – any other country

2013 – Chinese: $129 billion – Americans: $86 billion

How tourists spend money – changing

shopping – main reasons

More than 80% of Chinese tourists – shopping important

56% of Middle Eastern tourists, 48% of Russians

c Work with a partner. Using the notes, write a paragraph about Chinese tourism.

d Compare your paragraph with other students. Were your paragraphs similar?

5 READING EXTENSION

a Read part of an article from a website about tourism and answer the questions. Which of the trends below are increasing and which are decreasing? Write *I* or *D*.

1 the number of Chinese tourists going abroad _____
2 the rate of growth in Chinese tourism _____
3 the amount of money Chinese tourists spend on shopping _____
4 the number of Chinese tourists travelling in large groups _____
5 Chinese tourists' interest in the culture of the countries they visit _____
6 the number of Chinese families travelling together _____

b What does the article tell us about these things?

1 the Chinese middle class
2 visa restrictions
3 housing costs in China
4 local food
5 shopping malls
6 Chinese people living abroad
7 families booking holidays

What's changing in Chinese tourism?

In recent years, the number of Chinese tourists has grown at an incredible rate, so will it continue to grow in the future?

The short answer is 'yes'.

The longer answer is that it will continue to increase but perhaps a little more slowly than before. Mastercard's 'Future of Outbound Travel' report suggests an average growth of 8.5% each year between now and 2021. China's rising middle class, earning between US$10,000 and US$30,000, will drive an increase in tourism in the coming years. McKinsey & Company predict that more than three quarters of the population will be middle class by 2022. Also, cheaper and more frequent flights as well as fewer visa restrictions are making it easier and more convenient for Chinese travellers to explore the world.

Here are some recent (and growing) trends.

1 Less shopping and more experiences

Previously, Chinese travellers shopped a lot during their trips abroad because of large price differences and better quality and design of products, but this is gradually changing. Also, the cost of housing and education in China is rising, which means that younger travellers have less money to spend.

Just like tourists from other countries, Chinese travellers are becoming more interested in spending money on good local food and on experiencing the local culture, rather than on things.

2 Growing numbers of independent Chinese travellers

A few years ago most Chinese tourists went on organised bus tours that took them to 'top sights' and shopping malls. Now more travellers want to visit less well-known places and they want to find their way independently, not in a large group. As travel becomes easier for Chinese tourists, we can expect more independent travellers who will visit a destination in small groups, with family or friends.

3 Family travel is increasing

Over the last year, there has not only been an increase in travel abroad by Chinese tourists, but also in family travel. According to Forbes Magazine, there was an 18% rise in bookings made by families of up to four members for travel during this holiday season compared to last year. These trips are often paid for by young Chinese professionals living abroad who are flying their relatives out to spend the holidays, or else by older travellers who are taking their families on holidays abroad. More and more families are also going on holidays which they organise themselves, looking for quality time for the whole family instead of going on fast tours of tourist sites and shops.

ACADEMIC SKILLS PLUS

Economics: How people spend money

Listening skills: Noticing lecture structure;
Listening for key points
Speaking skills: Discourse markers to show
contrast

1 SPEAKING

a 🗨 You win £500 in a competition, but you can only use the money in one of two ways:

1 buy a brand new tablet
2 go on a holiday weekend somewhere interesting

Choose one option and say why you chose it.

b 🗨 Do you think most people prefer to spend money on things they can own or on experiences? Why?

2 LISTENING 1

a ▶3.1 Listen to the first part of a lecture. The lecturer asks some people the question in 1a. What do most people answer?

b ▶3.1 Skills focus Noticing the structure of a lecture

Listen again and answer the questions.
1 What is the order of the information in the excerpt? The lecturer …
   a asks a personal question.
   b says what he's going to talk about next.
   c gives other people's answers.
2 Match these expressions to a–c in question 1.
   i) 'many people I talk to say …' _____
   ii) 'how would you like …' _____
   iii) I'd like to focus on …' _____

> **STUDY SKILLS: QUESTIONS IN LECTURES**
> 1 Why does the lecturer ask a question?
> 2 Does he expect students in the lecture to answer?
> 3 Do lecturers often ask questions in this way?

3 LISTENING 2

a 🗨 Discuss the questions.
1 Why do you think remembering a holiday experience makes people happy?
2 What other kind of experiences can people buy?

b ▶3.2 Listen to the second part of the lecture. What answers does the lecturer give to the questions in 3a?

c Read the key points from the lecture. Listen and choose the correct words.

1 People are usually happier about spending money on an experience *before / after* paying for it.
2 New things we buy easily become *boring / broken*.
3 Experiences make us happy because *we share them / they're fun*.
4 Paying a person to do a *difficult / boring* job is another kind of experience you can buy.
5 In the Canadian experiment *all / some* students were told to spend money on someone else.
6 The result of the experiment shows we're happier when we are *generous / poor*.
7 The amount of money we give away *is / isn't* important if we want to feel happy.

d  **CRITICAL THINKING**
    APPLYING NEW KNOWLEDGE

If giving money away can make us happy, what's going to make us happiest – giving it to people we know or to people we don't know? Give your opinion and say why.

4 LANGUAGE FOCUS Language of contrast

a Read the examples from the presentation. Complete the sentences with the words in the box.

> however   but   yet   on the other hand   although

1 Maybe you could finally afford to buy that nice new tablet computer you've been thinking about. _____, £500 might mean you could have a holiday weekend away somewhere interesting.
2 They say it's something they can use for a long time, _____ a few people think it's better to spend money on the holiday, the experience, because it's something they will always remember.
3 … in other words, they stop being interesting. _____, experiences are things we do with other people …
4 So spending money on doing things is important, _____ it's not the only way of buying an experience.
5 Some students were told to spend the money on themselves _____ others were told to spend the money on another person.

b ▶3.3 Listen and check your answers.

c Are these sentences true or false? Write T or F.

The words in 4a …
1 join two ideas together.
2 introduce a second idea that is the same as the first idea.
3 introduce an idea that is different from the first idea.

d Answer the questions.
1 Which words/expressions are at the beginning of a sentence?
2 Which words/expressions are in the middle of a sentence?

e Match ideas 1–5 with a–e. Use a different word or expression from 4a each time. Different answers are possible.

1 Giving money away can make us happy.
2 It seems like a good idea to spend money on small experiences every week or month.
3 Real experiences are important for happiness.
4 Asking someone to do your housework can make you happy.
5 Giving away small amounts of money sounds like a good idea.

a Many people say that buying objects like books and tablets can also give you a kind of experience.
b If the cleaner does it badly, you may feel annoyed.
c Many people can't afford it.
d If you do it all the time, it could become expensive.
e You might also want to save for a bigger, more expensive experience in the future.

f 💬 Compare your answers in 4e with a partner. Are your answers the same?

5 PRONUNCIATION Tones

a ▶3.4 Listen to the examples from the presentation. Does the tone in the underlined words go up or down?

1 They say it's something they can use for a long time, yet a few people think it's better to spend money on the holiday, the experience, because it's something they will always remember.
2 Some students were told to spend the money on themselves, but others were told to spend the money on another person.

b ▶3.5 Listen to these sentences. Which syllable is stressed in the underlined word/expression?

1 Maybe you could finally afford to buy that nice new tablet computer you've been thinking about. On the other hand, £500 might mean you could have a holiday weekend away somewhere interesting.
2 In other words, they stop being interesting. However, experiences are things we do with other people.
3 So spending money on doing things is important, although it's not the only way of buying an experience.

c ▶3.5 Listen again and answer the questions.

1 Does the tone on the stressed syllable go up or down?
2 What happens after the stressed syllable? Does the next syllable … ?
a stay up   b stay down   c go down

6 SPEAKING

a Think of at least two of the following situations:
1 an object that you bought
2 an experience you paid for
3 money you gave to someone you know
4 money you gave to a charity

Make notes on the two situations by answering some of these questions.
- what did you buy / pay for? Why?
- who was involved in the experience?
- who or what did you give money to? Why?
- how did you feel before and after?

b 💬 Tell your partner about your situations. Use expressions from 4a when you speak.

c 💬 Discuss each other's situations. Were they similar? Did you both feel the same way after?

1 SPEAKING AND VOCABULARY

a 💬 Discuss the questions.

1 Do you or your friends take selfies and put them online? Why / Why not?
2 What kind of selfies do you look at? Ones of famous people? Or ones of your family and friends?
3 What makes a selfie interesting?

b Match the <u>underlined</u> words in the sentences to the definitions a and b.

1 I like to have a cup of tea in bed before I get up. This is part of my morning <u>ritual</u>.
2 When you study a new language, it helps if you understand the society and <u>culture</u> of that language.

> a the habits of a group of people and the things they believe
> b an activity or set of actions that are always done in the same way at the same time.

c 💬 Look at the definitions.

1 *personal rituals* special habits that you have
2 *traditional social rituals* typical things that only people from your country do and they have done them for a long time

Think of an example of a personal ritual and a traditional social ritual. Tell you partner.

2 LISTENING 1

a ▶4.1 Listen to the first part of Deniz's presentation. Which is the best summary of what she says, 1 or 2?

1 She explains what a ritual is and talks about how selfies are rituals that are part of modern culture. She gives an example of a social ritual from her country where they use the national flag.
2 She gives a definition of rituals and explains how selfies are common social rituals. She gives an example of young women taking selfies at weddings.

b ▶4.1 Deniz talks about the three ideas below. Listen again and add extra information for each idea.

1 different ways of looking at modern culture: _____
2 a family ritual: _____
3 a wedding ritual in Turkey: _____

c 💬 Tell your partner about typical wedding rituals in your country.

3 LISTENING 2

a ▶4.2 In the second part of the presentation, Deniz talks about these topics. Check the meaning of the <u>underlined</u> words with your teacher. Listen for the correct order of topics 1–6.

1 the place where people take a selfie
2 old paintings that are <u>self-portraits</u>
3 uploading a selfie to a social media website
4 a million selfies every day
5 the way people <u>pose</u> for a selfie
6 rituals are <u>inherited</u> and pass from one generation to the next

b ▶4.2 Below are details that can be added to the main points in 3a. Listen again and match them to the main points.

a showing a picture of yourself is not a new idea _____
b finding out what people think of your selfie _____
c people between the age of 18 and 24 _____
d the way you stand and the way you hold your smartphone _____
e Browne says this in 'Profiles of Popular Culture' (2005) _____
f 'see where I have been' or 'see how I live' _____

c 🧠 CRITICAL THINKING
USING MIND MAPS TO SUMMARISE INFORMATION

Add key words and phrases to the two mind maps to create summaries for the whole presentation.

can be personal or social

way to say 'this is me'

RITUALS

SELFIES

4 PRONUNCIATION Pausing

a ▶**4.3** Below are the final two sentences. / shows where Deniz makes a small pause. Listen and check. Which version below shows the way that Deniz pauses?

1 Some people say it means / we are narcissistic in other words / that we love ourselves / too much. / But other people think it's just / a way of saying 'this is who I am / this is me.'

2 Some people say / it means we are narcissistic / in other words / that we love ourselves too much. / But other people think / it's just a way of saying / 'this is who I am / this is me.'

b Answer the questions.

1 Why does Deniz use these small pauses when speaking?

2 Why does Deniz put a strong stress on 'some' in the first sentence and 'other' in the second sentence?

c In pairs, take turns saying the correct example in 4a. Use correct pauses and stress.

5 LANGUAGE FOCUS Defining expressions

a In the first sentences in 4a, Deniz explains the meaning of the word 'narcissistic'. Answer the questions.

1 Does Deniz think everyone will understand the word 'narcissistic'?

2 Does she think it's useful or important for them to understand this word?

3 What expression introduces her definition?

b ▶**4.4** Listen to the examples. Put one word in each gap to complete an expression that introduces a definition.

1 _____ exactly _____ _____ _____ _____ the word 'ritual'?

2 … rituals are activities that are inherited _____ _____ one generation passes a ritual to the next generation.

3 … how they are going to pose for the camera. _____ _____ _____ _____ the way they hold their body and the look they have on their face.

c Add one of the expressions in 5a or 5b to the examples below.

1 People always want positive social media feedback, _____ others like pictures you have put online.

2 Selfies can create a false impression, _____ , they show a life that is not the same as the real life someone lives.

3 _____ a personal ritual? Something that we do every day.

4 People often use selfies to try and fit in. _____ they are a way to show you belong to a group of people you know and like.

d 💬 Work in pairs. Use the role cards from your teacher. Look at the <u>underlined</u> words and think about how you can define them. You can use the definitions at the end of the card to help you.

e 💬 Read the text on your card to a partner. Add in definitions for the <u>underlined</u> words using expressions from 5a and 5b.

> **STUDY SKILLS: DEFINING NEW WORDS AND IDEAS IN A PRESENTATION**
>
> 1 When you give a presentation, will the people who listen always know what you are talking about?
>
> 2 How can you help listeners understand new words or ideas they are not familiar with?

6 SPEAKING

a Work alone. Think of a topic you have studied or a hobby or interest you have. You are going to tell other students about your topic. Use the questions to make notes.

1 What is the topic?

2 Why are you interested in it?

3 What are the main ideas or key points about the topic that might be interesting to other people?

4 Have you read any books or articles about the topic? What information was in them?

5 Do you know any interesting or surprising information that other people don't know about the topic?

b What specific words or expressions will you need to talk about your topic? Write the word(s) and a simple definition.

c 💬 Work in pairs or small groups. Tell each other about your topic and use defining expressions when you need to explain words or ideas. As you listen to your partner, think of a question you can ask them after.

Unit 5 Study and work

1 SPEAKING

a 💬 In your country, is the cost of a university education going up or down? Why?

b 💬 Think about students' expenses. What are the most important things they need to spend money on? Put the costs below in order from 1 (= most important) to 8 (= least important).

- [ ] food
- [ ] course fees
- [ ] accommodation
- [ ] books for study
- [ ] clothes
- [ ] transport
- [ ] exercise/sport
- [ ] social activities

c 💬 Compare your answers. What are the differences? How easy is it to decide what is most important?

2 VOCABULARY Finance

a Match the words in **bold** in 1–5 to definitions a–e.

1 When there is **inflation**, the cost of everything goes up.
2 He has so much **debt** that he'll never be able to pay it all back.
3 In the UK young people from **low-income** families often cannot afford to go to university.
4 Her exam results were so good she got a small student **grant** that she didn't have to pay back.
5 She got a student **loan** to cover the cost of her course fees.

a used to describe people who do not earn a lot of money _____
b money that is given away by an organisation or government for a special reason _____
c a general rise in how much we pay for things _____
d the money you borrow from a bank or a person and have to pay back _____
e something, usually money, that you owe a person or an organisation _____

b 💬 Think about your country and discuss the questions.

1 Do students in your country leave university with a lot of debt?
2 Is it possible for students to get study grants or do they need to get loans from the government?
3 How easy is it for students from low-income families to study at university?

3 READING

a Read the introduction to an article on page 17 that discusses university students who do part-time work. Match summaries a–c to paragraphs 1–3.

a How part-time work affects students' study _____
b The costs of studying at university _____
c Why some students work part-time _____

b Read the introduction again and add information in note form to the key points in each paragraph.

> **Paragraph 1**
>
> 1 course fees __*price has gone up in past 15 years*__
> 2 student costs _____
> 3 student loans _____
>
> **Paragraph 2**
>
> 4 three reasons for working part-time
> _____
> 5 work experience
> _____
>
> **Paragraph 3**
>
> 6 ways part-time work affects study
> _____
> 7 financial reasons
> _____
> 8 career / intellectual reasons
> _____

c 🧠 CRITICAL THINKING
RECOGNISING AND COLLECTING INFORMATION

Discuss the questions.

1 In 3a did you need to understand … ?
   a in detail
   b just the main ideas
2 In 3b did you need to understand … ?
   a in detail
   b just the main ideas
3 What's the connection between the main ideas and the details? Choose the best answer.
   In a paragraph …
   a there is usually one main point as well as detailed information that supports the main point.
   b there are two or three main points followed by one sentence that gives detailed information.

PART-TIME WORK:
What's the academic cost?
Introduction

1 In many countries, the cost of a university education has increased slowly in the past fifteen years or so. In the UK, course fees have gone up in price because universities need more money to offer a range of courses and pay for quality teaching. Students have to pay for their living costs and inflation means the price of rent and food has increased. They may come from low-income families who cannot afford to support their children at university. Students can get loans to help pay for their living costs, but this means they leave university with a lot of debt. Their solution to the problem of an expensive university education has been to do part-time work while they study.

2 Earning extra money is an important aim of part-time work, but students often give other reasons for working while they study. A recent report in the UK (Jewell 2014) showed that the three main reasons for working part-time were 1) to pay for social and free-time expenses; 2) to help pay for living costs; 3) to not get into too much debt during their study. There are also some students who do part-time work because they want to get useful work experience while they are studying. They believe this will make it easier for them to find a job when they graduate from university. Students in this category often look for part-time jobs that are related to the career they would like to follow after they graduate.

3 The fact that many students work part-time raises the question of whether this affects their academic performance or not. Students' different reasons for doing part-time work mean their study is affected in different ways. It depends on why they are working part-time, how much work they do and what kind of work they do. Students who need to work part-time for financial reasons will often have study problems and get lower grades. However, this does not happen when students do part-time work that is related to their career objectives. A study in Russia suggested that for these students there is little negative impact on their studies (Yanbarisova 2015). The same study also suggested that when students do part-time work that is more intellectual, it can have a positive effect on their learning.

4 LANGUAGE FOCUS Topic sentences

a In paragraph 1 the main idea was *The costs of studying at university*. Read the paragraph again and answer the questions.
   1 Which sentence tells us what the paragraph is about?
   2 What information do the other sentences give?

b Most paragraphs have one sentence that tells us the main idea of the paragraph. This is called the *topic sentence*. Below are the main ideas for paragraphs 2 and 3. Find the topic sentences. The topic sentence is not always the first one.
   Paragraph 2: Why some students work part-time
   Paragraph 3: How part-time work affects students' study

c Read the paragraph below. Choose the best topic sentence to go at the beginning, 1 or 2.
   1 The increase in part-time work has meant less free time for students.
   2 The increase in students' part-time work has resulted in time management problems.

Students often have to make difficult decisions about how they organise their time while at university. In a survey done in the UK, many students said they needed to think very carefully about the balance between part-time work and study. If they work more, they have fewer money problems, but this can have a negative effect on their study. They also said they have less time for free-time activities and hobbies. This means they are always working and studying and never have time to relax.

d Write a topic sentence for this paragraph. Note: *they* refers to students.

First of all, they should think about the pay. If they can only work 10 to 15 hours a week, they need to earn as much as possible. Another point they need to consider is the location of the job. It should be near the place they live so they do not pay a lot of money in transport costs. Finally, the work hours are important because they need to be at times when students do not have lectures. It is often easy to find work as a shop assistant or a waiter, but often these jobs do not pay a lot of money, are far away and have unfriendly timetables. There are other jobs that pay more and are often more convenient. For example, a student can become a part-time social media assistant for a company. The pay is good, the job can be done at home and students can work when they want.

STUDY SKILLS: READING TOPIC SENTENCES
When you are reading, you can look for the topic sentence in a paragraph.
1 If you only read topic sentences, will this give you a general or detailed understanding of the text?
2 Will it mean that you read quickly or slowly?

5 WRITING

a Use the notes below to write a paragraph with a topic sentence. The paragraph reports on three universities and the reasons why students failed. Use the past simple to report the reasons.

Other reasons for poor academic results
- three universities in (*country*)
- different reasons for failing
- some students – study wrong subject – course work difficult – bad grade
- also – family / emotional problems – negative effect
- small number of students – not motivated – didn't keep up with course work – failed

b Read your partner's paragraph and topic sentence. Are they similar?

6 READING EXTENSION

a Read the newspaper article about part-time student work. Are these sentences true or false?

1 Students in the UK worry about not finding a job as soon as they finish studying.
2 Most students follow the suggestion of universities to work between 10 and 15 hours a week.
3 Miranda didn't have a lot of free time when she was studying at university.
4 Zach's experience of working part-time has been positive.
5 James thinks that trying to have an active social life when you study is quite stressful.
6 The National Union of Students suggests that students shouldn't work too much.

b Read the article again and answer the questions.

1 What three points of view about part-time student work are given in the article?
2 What conclusion does it reach about the topic?
3 Do you agree with the conclusion?

The realities of balancing employment with your studies

The cost of some university degrees in the UK is £27,000 and that's just for the course fees. What's more, students know that having a degree doesn't mean that you will definitely get a job and start earning money after you finish studying. As a result, students feel that they have to have a part-time job when they study. But how well does it work to mix a part-time job as a shop assistant with studying for a degree?

A survey in 2014 found that 57% of students have a part-time job while they are at university. Nine out of ten of these people work as many as 20 hours per week. However, most universities suggest that students only do between 10 and 15 hours part-time work a week during an academic term.

Miranda Jones, who used to study English Literature and Film Studies, worked in a supermarket when she was studying. On average she worked between 15 and 20 hours per week.

She said: 'If I didn't work then I couldn't afford to live. My job paid for food and transport. My student loan was only enough for the rent on my flat. I really didn't have much of a social life – I was too busy studying or working or sleeping!'

Miranda believes her part-time work had a negative effect on her academic performance. She added: 'I think my grades would have been better if I hadn't worked. But I couldn't afford to study at university without my part-time job.'

Zach Fryer, a third year Psychology student, has a job with the Student Union at his university. He hasn't had any problems balancing his job with his studies.

He said: 'It has meant I can live more comfortably and I can afford a social life without worrying how much I'm spending. Working for the Student Union has also been a great way to meet people and make new friends.'

Zach also said that having a job with the Student Union made it possible for him to choose when he worked, and during busy times like the exam season, he could reduce his working hours.

Students at Oxford University aren't allowed to work part-time during term time unless there's a special reason. James Lutton, a second year History student at Oxford, believes this has a positive impact on students.

He said: 'If the university can make sure that everyone can afford to study full-time, then it means your study will be less stressful. It means you are free to really focus on your study and the experience of being at university as a whole. There's no problem getting behind in your study and you can have a social life as well.'

James added that Oxford has shorter, eight-week terms so this gives students the opportunity to work during the holidays.

It doesn't matter if you're talking about part-time work during term time or full-time work during the holidays, the economic reality for students is some extra income is essential. But how well does this work match academic study?

Research that was done by the National Union of Students showed that most people agreed there were positive benefits when students work part-time. However, it's important that students have a good work/study balance. The University of Ulster encourages students to look for work opportunities when they're studying. They often let students get extra study credits when they work in a part-time job.

If the aim of a degree is to prepare students for the working world, then perhaps more students would benefit from this kind of support.

Unit 6 Phobias

1 SPEAKING

a 💬 How do you feel about the things in the pictures?

- i have no problem with this
- i don't really like it but it doesn't bother me too much
- i don't like this at all

Do you know other people who don't like these things?

b 💬 Fear of things like these are *phobias*. What other things do people sometimes have phobias about? Make a list (use a dictionary to help).

flying

spiders

2 LISTENING 1

a Look at the three definitions of a phobia. Which do you think is the best one?

A phobia is …
1 a sudden fear which makes you unable to think normally.
2 a strong fear that something terrible will happen to you.
3 an irrational fear of something which is not really dangerous.

b ▶️6.1 Listen to three students discussing a homework assignment on the question: *What is a phobia?*

1 Which definition in 2a do they give?
2 Andy and Lucy talk about types of phobia. Do they have … ?
  a the same answers   b different answers
3 Are agoraphobia and claustrophobia … ?
  a almost the same   b quite different.

c ▶️6.1 Add the phrases below to the gaps in Andy's and Lucy's notes. Then listen again to check.

air travel	crowded places	speaking in public	spiders

Andy: Kinds of phobia
1 things that you can avoid, e.g. ¹_____
2 things that are part of your normal life (you can't avoid them), e.g. being in crowds

Lucy: Phobias – main categories
1 simple phobias, about things, e.g. spiders, ²_____
2 social phobias, e.g. ³_____
3 agoraphobia = being in a place where you can't escape, e.g. open spaces, ⁴_____

ACADEMIC SKILLS PLUS

Psychology: Fear

Listening skills: Identifying points from a group discussion; Identifying turn-taking strategies
Speaking skills: Turn-taking in a discussion

being in a high place

being in a crowded train

d Look again at the phobias in your list in 1b. Which categories do you think they belong to?

3 PRONUNCIATION Connected speech

a ▶️6.2 Listen to three short extracts from the recording.

1 Which words are stressed in each extract?
2 In which extract(s) do you hear these words or phrases?
  a isn't actually   c isn't it   e scared of
  b being   d about

b ▶️6.2 Listen again. What do you notice about the words and phrases in question 2 in 3a?

1 the speaker says them *quickly / slowly*
2 the vowel sounds are mainly *short / long*
3 you *can / can't* hear all the sounds
4 words *are clearly separate / often sound like one word*

c Here are some sentences you will hear in the next part of the recording. How do you think the speaker will say them? Which words do you think will be … ?

- stressed   • said more quickly

1 So what about how common they are?
2 It turns out they're very common.
3 First of all you can't control the symptoms.

d ▶️6.3 Listen and check how the speaker says them.

4 LISTENING 2

a Look at these sentences about phobias. Do you think they are true or false?

1 Millions of people suffer from phobias.
2 Men suffer from phobias more than women.
3 Phobias mainly affect older people.

b ▶6.4 The students discuss these questions:

• how common are phobias?
• what are the symptoms of a phobia?

Listen and check your answers to 4a.

c ▶6.4 Listen again. Which of these symptoms do they mention?

1 Your mouth feels dry.
2 It's difficult to breathe.
3 Your face goes white.
4 You start crying.
5 You know there's no reason to be afraid, but it doesn't help.
6 You feel hot and start sweating.
7 You want to run away, but you can't move.

d 🧠 CRITICAL THINKING
EXPLORING CAUSES AND REASONS

Here are three explanations for phobias. Which of them do you think ... ?

• are definitely true
• may be true but don't really explain phobias
• aren't true at all

1 'Many phobias make sense. For example, some spiders and snakes are dangerous. Flying in an airplane is unnatural and you can easily die. So phobias aren't irrational at all.'

2 'Phobias start with your parents. For example, if you see that your parents are afraid of spiders, you learn to be afraid of them too. Or if you parents tell you not to touch a spider, you will start to be afraid of it.'

3 'Phobias start when you are a child. For example, maybe you were locked in a cupboard when you were a child. You were very scared but later you forgot that it happened. But you still have a fear of dark places.'

5 LANGUAGE FOCUS
Sharing ideas – taking turns

a Look at the expressions in the box. Which expressions mean ... ?

1 I want to speak – it's my turn.
2 Wait, I'm thinking.
3 You can speak now – it's your turn.

What did you have?   Shall I talk about that?
Go on, then.   Just a minute, I'll tell you.
Go ahead.   Can I say what I've got?
---

b Add one expression from the box in 5a in each gap. More than one answer may be possible.

1 **ANDY** OK, so let's start with the definition then. ____
  MIRA Well, um, I found the basic definition.

2 **LUCY** And then there's a third category which is – um, ____ ... Oh yeah, agoraphobia.

3 **ANDY** So what about how common they are? ____
  LUCY ____
  ANDY OK, well, in fact it turns out they're very common.

4 **LUCY** OK, sounds good. Let's talk about the symptoms ...
  MIRA Well, ____
  LUCY OK. Well, first of all you can't control the symptoms ...

c ▶6.5 Listen and check what the people said. Would more than one answer be possible?

d 💬 Practise these conversations. Use expressions from 5a for the parts in italics.

1 **A** OK, let's talk about fear of spiders. *(Ask B to speak.)*
  B *(Ask A to wait – you need to look at your notes.)*

2 **A** OK, let's do question 3, about symptoms. *(You want to answer.)*
  B *(Let A answer.)*

3 **A** OK, the next question – What is claustrophobia?
  B *(You want to answer.)*
  A *(Let B answer.)*

e 💬 Have the conversations again. This time, change roles and add one more line to the conversation.

STUDY SKILLS: SHARING IDEAS

In the discussion in 4b, the students share ideas and take turns to speak. Why is it a good idea to give everyone a chance to speak in a discussion? Choose the **most important** reason.

a It means everyone is involved
b It makes a good atmosphere in the class
c You can learn from other people
d You don't have to do so much work
e It helps the weaker students
---

6 SPEAKING

a 💬 Work in groups of three. You are going to have a discussion about phobias, answering these questions:

1 What is the definition of a phobia?
2 How common are phobias?
3 What are the symptoms of a phobia?
4 What common phobias are there?

b Prepare for the discussion and make a few notes.

• student A: Prepare answers to questions 1, 2 and 4.
• student B: Prepare answers to questions 1, 3 and 4.
• student C: Prepare answers to questions 2, 3 and 4.

c 💬 Share your answers to the questions and make sure you all take turns to speak. Use expressions from 5a.

Unit 7 Computer games

1 SPEAKING

a 💬 Did you play video or computer games when you were a child?

If so …

- what kind of games did you play?
- did you play mainly with friends or alone?

If not, why didn't you play them?

- because your parents didn't allow it
- because you didn't like them
- another reason

b 💬 Which opinion do you agree with? Why?

1 Parents should let children play computer games whenever they like.
2 Parents should let children play computer games but they should control what they play.
3 Parents should only let children play computer games for a short time every day.

3 READING

2 VOCABULARY

a Here are some words (1–7) from the reading text. Match them with the meanings a–g.

1 ☐ Many computer games are **repetitive.**
2 ☐ Some computer games are **violent**.
3 ☐ Children usually **interact** with each other when they play.
4 ☐ I said 'Hello' but she **ignored** me.
5 ☐ I get all my news from electronic **media**.
6 ☐ There are big **cognitive** differences between children of different ages.
7 ☐ Playing computer games is quite a recent **phenomenon**.

a communicate or talk together
b choose not to notice someone
c radio, TV, films, the internet, …
d something that exists or which you can see
e connected with how you think
f you do the same thing again and again
g may include killing or hurting people

Computer games as tools for play and social interaction

Most children enjoy playing computer games. However, parents often worry that if their children play computer games they will interact less with friends. Many people see this as a greater problem with boys than with girls. This is because boys often seem to enjoy games with non-stop high-speed action on the screen. The games in this category, which have been on the market for over 35 years, seem simple and repetitive, and many adults notice the violent elements in many of them. However, computer games are, after all, still games, and should be compared with other games. For example, look at table tennis. It is fast moving and repetitive, but very few people play it simply to win or to beat others. People play because it is a fun way to spend time together. In other words, it is all about play. If you watch a group of children playing a computer game, you will see that their interaction and behaviour are not all that different from those you will see around other games. The group closely follows the game and comments on its development and the performance of the player(s).

Children sometimes play computer games on their own – in the same way as they watch TV and read books on their own – as children often use media to pass the time when they are bored, just like adults. But there are very few children who would rather play computer games, watch TV or read books than spend time together with their friends and playmates. For children today, it is not a question of 'either …, or …'. Using media does not necessarily mean choosing to ignore friends – quite the opposite, in fact.

When children play computer games it is typical for them to do so in a group, and unless the surrounding environment prevents it, this group will consist of children of different ages – as is often the case in computer clubs. One reason these games are popular is that interest in them brings together different age groups. In this context, young children have the opportunity to have conversations with older children.

It is interesting that the age aspect is not only based on cognitive differences between the children. Young children can play very complicated computer games that were originally designed for much older children and so should be above their level. However, as the children consider it important to be part of the group, they develop the skills and knowledge necessary. Similarly, games intended for their own age group are often considered 'childish' and therefore of little or no interest.

The phenomenon of 'the group around the computer' also occurs with other media. Children often get together after school to watch online videos. They go to the cinema together, or they use TV series as the basis for games or as subject matter for conversations and social interaction.

These activities do not prevent contact with other children; they are integrated into children's games and social interaction. As we have seen, the media often become the 'tools' for games and are important for generating play situations.

a Read the article on page 21 and look at the sentences below. Which <u>three</u> sentences are main points in the article?

1 Children play computer games and other games in a similar way.
2 Most children find computer games more interesting than table tennis.
3 Playing computer games gives children a chance to learn from older children.
4 Many computer games aren't suitable for younger children.
5 Using media doesn't stop children playing and interacting together.

b Read the article again and <u>underline</u> the best answers.

1 Some parents don't like boys' computer games because they're often *boring / violent*.
2 Most children play table tennis *to win and score points / to have a good time together*.
3 Most children prefer to play computer games *alone / with friends*.
4 Children of different ages *often / rarely* play computer games together.
5 Younger children usually find complicated computer games *too difficult / interesting and fun*.
6 Computer games are like other kinds of media because they give children opportunities for *competition / being together*.

c **Skills focus** Main points and supporting details

Look at these sentences from the beginning of the article.
1 Boys often seem to enjoy action games with non-stop high-speed action on the screen.
2 The games in this category, which have been on the market for more than 35 years, seem simple and repetitive.

Which sentence … ?
a makes the main point about what games boys play
b adds to the main point and gives more information

d Here are some more examples. Without looking at the article, match the main points (1–5) and the supporting details (a–e). Then check in the text.

1 ☐ Computer games are, after all, still games, and should be compared with other games.
2 ☐ When children play computer games it is typical for them to do so in a group.
3 ☐ It is worth noting that the age aspect is not only based on cognitive differences between the children.
4 ☐ If you watch a group of children playing a computer game, you will see that their interaction and behaviour are not all that different from those you will see around other games.
5 ☐ The phenomenon of 'the group around the computer' is also to be found centred around other media.

a Children often get together after school to watch online videos.
b For example, look at table tennis. It is fast moving and repetitive, but very few people play it simply to win or to beat others.
c This group will consist of children of different ages – as is often the case in computer clubs or internet cafés.
d The group closely follows the game and comments on its development and the performance of the player(s).
e Young children can play very complicated computer games that were originally designed for much older children.

e Which sentences a–e … ?

1 help to explain the main point (x 2)
2 give an example to support the main point (x 2)
3 add an extra detail or more information (x 1)

f **CRITICAL THINKING**
GOING BEYOND THE TEXT

Do you think the skills children learn in computer games can also be useful for other things in their lives? Think about …

| sports | playing in teams | making decisions |
| concentrating | trying to win | |

4 LANGUAGE FOCUS
Referencing with *this* and *these*

a Look at the sentences from the article and discuss the questions.

> A Parents often worry that if their children play computer games they will interact less with friends. Many people see **this** as a greater problem with boys than with girls.
>
> B Boys often seem to enjoy action games with non-stop high-speed action on the screen. The games in **this category** seem simple and repetitive.
>
> C When children play computer games it is typical for them to do so in a group. One reason **these games** are popular is that interest in them brings together different age groups.

1 What is the difference between *this* and *these*?
2 Do the words in **bold** refer … ?
  a back to an earlier idea
  b forward to the next idea
3 What do the words in **bold** in A–C refer to? Choose from the list below.
  a games
  b computer games
  c action games
  d repetitive games
  e children playing games
  f children playing computer games instead of interacting with friends

b Find one more example in the article of …

1 the word *this* on its own
2 a phrase with *this* + noun
3 a phrase with *these* + noun

What do they refer to?

c Add *this* or *these* and a word from the box in each gap. Then answer the question below.

activities	age	pictures	problem

1 Many of today's children have almost no contact with nature. One solution to _____ _____ is to arrange school trips to the countryside.
2 After-school clubs provide opportunities for children to play sports and to make things. _____ _____ help children to learn how to work together in a team.
3 Many children start school when they are five or six. At _____ _____ , children learn best through playing games.
4 Most children use phones to take selfies and they can instantly share _____ _____ with their friends.

In which sentence could you also use the word *this* on its own?

5 WRITING

a Read the outline of a paragraph about children and technology. The main ideas are given, and the supporting details (in brackets) are in note form.

> • children today are part of a digital generation. (surrounded by technology – internet, mobile phones, tablets, computers)
>
> • for some parents this can be a problem. (children understand new technology – better than parents – hard to control)
>
> • some parents believe that using technology stops children learning other skills. (research: young children – 50% can use a smartphone – 20% can ride a bike)
>
> • however, technology can also help children to learn skills and grow up faster. (leave school – better skills in technology than parents)
>
> • parents need to make sure their children are using technology sensibly, but this doesn't always happen. (interview with primary schoolchildren: 15% – parents never check; over 30% – internet in bedroom)

b Work in pairs.

1 Decide how you could expand the notes to make sentences.
2 Together, write the complete paragraph. Include the main ideas and supporting details, and add any further ideas you like.

c Compare your paragraph with another pair. How are they the same? How are they different?

STUDY SKILLS: EXPANDING NOTES

When you expand notes into sentences, what kind of words do you need to add? Choose from this list.

• nouns and verbs
• words like *is, are, will, was*
• words like *the, a, their*
• pronouns
• linking words like *but, and, so, because*
• adjectives

6 READING EXTENSION

a Read the article. Choose the question which gives the <u>best</u> summary of the article.

1 Should toddlers play with tablets?
2 How does technology affect children's development?
3 How quickly do young children learn to use technology?

b The article refers to two different sources:
- the American Academy of Pediatrics (AAP)
- Emma Asprey (EA)

Which source would agree with these opinions? Write *AAP* or *EA*.

1 Children can use technology and also interact with people – it's not a problem. _____
2 Children who use technology interact less with other people. _____
3 We should teach children how to use technology in a positive way. _____
4 Technology can help children develop important skills. _____
5 Using digital devices can be harmful for young children. _____

c Think about these questions.

1 Which of the two sources do you think the writer agrees with more?
2 Which do you agree with?

How young is too young for technology?

Is there really a problem with toddlers playing with tablets? After all, if books really are becoming old-fashioned in the classroom, surely younger children should start with technology as early as possible?

Recent research has shown that, by the time they start school, 70 per cent of children can already use a laptop, tablet or smart phone. And another survey showed that 47 per cent of parents think it's important for a child to be familiar with technology before school, while 17 per cent of children under three actually own their own smart phone or tablet.

So is this a problem? Some experts believe it is. The American Academy of Pediatrics, for example, says that children under 2 should not be given digital devices to play with and that pre-school children should not watch television or use digital devices for more than two hours a day. One reason for this is that 80% of brain development takes place between the ages of nought to three. If children of that age spend too much time using technology instead of playing with other children, it could affect their behaviour and make it harder to interact with other people or express feelings when they grow up.

But Emma Asprey, Senior Lecturer at Bath Spa University in England, doesn't agree with this view. She believes that technology doesn't always have a negative effect on children's communication skills – in fact it can add to the many ways in which children naturally communicate.

She also believes that as children reach secondary school age they need to know how to use the internet to find information accurately; they also need to know how to use social networks for learning rather than simply for chatting to friends. Technology, if it is used in the right way, can help learners to be more independent and can encourage them to find out things for themselves.

Children who have grown up with this technology from a young age will be in a better position to make use of technological skills. However, this needs to be balanced with reading, writing, playing with real toys and playing outdoors.

One thing seems certain – young children learn to use new technology very quickly and soon become confident in using it. Tablets in particular are perfect for very young children because they don't need to learn to use a keyboard or mouse. So instead of discouraging it, it may be better to see this as an opportunity for learning in the same way as the books, toys and games that children have always grown up with.

Unit 8   Selling music

1 SPEAKING

a 🗨 Ask your partner these questions.

1 How do you listen to music? Do you … ?
   - buy CDs, cassettes or vinyl records
   - stream music
   - buy and download music
   - watch music online or on TV
   - listen to music on the radio
2 How much money do you think you spend on music every month?
3 Think about yourself five years ago. How has the way you buy and listen to music changed?

2 LISTENING 1

a Skills focus Predicting what you will hear

Marcus is going to talk about music and digital media. You will hear five extracts from Marcus's presentation. In Part 1 Marcus introduces the topic. What do you think he will talk about?

▶️ 8.1 Listen to Part 1 and check your answers.

b In Parts 2 and 3, Marcus says the words and phrases in the boxes. What do you think he will say?

Part 2

2003	Myspace	upload	share	big names

Part 3

unknown musician	digital distributor
Amazon and Spotify	audience

▶️ 8.2 Listen to Parts 2 and 3 and check your ideas.

c In Part 4, Marcus says online distribution is better for music fans than it is for musicians. Why do you think that is?

▶️ 8.3 Listen to Part 4 and check your answer.

d Think about the topic of the presentation. What do you think Marcus's conclusion will be?

▶️ 8.4 Listen and check.

> **STUDY SKILLS: PREDICTING AND GUESSING**
>
> When we start listening to a talk or lecture, you can often guess some of what the speaker will say.
>
> 1 Why is it useful to try to do this?
> 2 How can you use these things to help you predict?
>   - the title of the talk
>   - the speaker's introduction
>   - presentation slides

3 LISTENING 2

a After the presentation, the other students ask these three questions.

1 Is Spotify a distributor?
2 How much does Spotify pay the artist when their music is played?
3 Has music got better, or is there just more of it?

What do you think Marcus's answers will be?

b ▶️ 8.5 Listen and check.

c 🧠 CRITICAL THINKING
   MATCHING WHAT YOU HEAR WITH YOUR OWN OPINION

Discuss Marcus's answer to question 3.

1 Does he seem to have a clear opinion?
2 Do you agree with his answers? What would your answers be?

4 LANGUAGE FOCUS
Clarifying and asking questions

a ▶8.6 Listen to the students' comments and questions again. Add one word to each expression.

AMANDA

1 **You** _____ digital distributors have contacts with companies like Spotify.
2 **I don't quite** _____ **that**.

PAULA

3 **I was** _____ … How much does Spotify pay the artist?
4 **Do you** _____ **anything about that?**

CARLA

5 **You** _____ that there are now thousands of people putting music online.
6 **What do you** _____ **about that?**

b Which of the expressions in bold can you use … ?

a to talk about something the speaker said (x2)
b to ask for an opinion or more information (x2)
c to show you don't understand (x1)
d to introduce a question (x1)

c Here are some more students' questions. Add a suitable expression from 4a in each gap. More than one answer may be possible.

1 I _____ – how are online distributors different from companies like Sony? _____ that?
2 You _____ Lily Allen used MySpace. Do you know of any other artists who used it?
3 You _____ musicians use digital distributors. How do they use them exactly? I _____.
4 You _____ most musicians don't make money.
   I _____ – what _____? Do you think that's fair?

d Read out your questions to other students. Did you use the same expressions?

5 PRONUNCIATION Unstressed words

a ▶8.7 Listen again to expressions 3, 4 and 6 in 4a.

1 Which words have the main stress?
2 Are the words in the box … ?
   a stressed   b not stressed

I	was	do	about

3 How does the speaker say the words?
   a slowly and with long sounds
   b quickly and with short sounds

b 💬 Practise saying the expressions quietly to yourself. Then say them aloud to your partner.

6 SPEAKING

a Prepare a short talk (about 1–2 minutes) based on the questions you discussed in 1a. Choose two or three of these topics and make a few notes:

• what kind of music do you listen to and what music do/don't you like?
• how do you listen to music (CDs, vinyl records, streaming, etc.)?
• when do you listen to music?
• how much money do you spend on music?
• have your music listening habits changed in the last five years?

b 💬 Work in groups of four or five. Take it in turns to give your talk.

1 Speaker: Give your talk.
2 Listeners: After the talk, each prepare <u>one</u> question to ask the speaker. Use expressions from 4a.
3 Listeners: Ask your questions.
   Speaker: Try to answer the listeners' questions.

ACADEMIC SKILLS PLUS

Applied linguistics: Bilingual education

Listening skills: Listening for main and supporting ideas
Speaking skills: Making main points

1 SPEAKING

a 💬 Tell each other about a language that you don't know at all, but would like to learn. What's the language? Why would you like to learn it?

b 💬 Read the definition of *bilingual education programmes* and discuss the questions.

> **bilingual education programmes** mean that high school students study subjects like history, mathematics and science in their mother tongue and a foreign language.

1 Was there a bilingual education programme at your high school?
2 If there was, what did you think of studying in this way? If there wasn't, would you have liked to study in a bilingual programme? Why / Why not?
3 What are the benefits of being bilingual? Talk about the following things:
   • university study
   • work
   • social opportunities
   • travel
   • developing special skills

2 LISTENING

a ▶️9.1 You will hear a podcast discussion with two experts on bilingual education: Jennifer May and Bruno Monti. They talk about ideas 1–7 below. Who talks about each idea? Listen and put *J* or *B* beside each idea.

1 It's easier to communicate with people from other countries in the modern world. _____
2 Bilingual people are better at cultural communication. _____
3 Bilingual people are more self-confident. _____
4 Bilingual people have a greater interest in communicating with other people. _____
5 Bilingual people are good at finding answers to problems. _____
6 Bilingual people are able to remember new ideas. _____
7 Old bilingual people have fewer problems with memory. _____

b Match points a–g with the ideas (1–7) in 2a.

a They can understand people from different backgrounds. _____
b They have met the challenge of learning a second language. _____
c IT and travel make it possible to get in touch with people who speak other languages. _____
d It's something they can do in two languages so they can do it well. _____
e They are very open and look for communication opportunities. _____
f They can use new information and it helps with learning. _____
g This can help society save money. _____

c ▶️9.1 Listen and check your answers.

d 🧠 CRITICAL THINKING
DISTINGUISHING BETWEEN DIFFERENT KINDS OF INFORMATION

Discuss the questions.

1 What is the difference between the information in the sentences in 2a and the sentences in 2b?
2 How do they relate to each other?
3 In the discussion, the information is spoken language. Can we organise information in a similar way in academic writing?

3 LANGUAGE FOCUS Making main points

a In each example, underline two words that show the idea is a main point in the discussion. The first one is done for you.

1 Yes, of course the <u>major benefit</u> of bilingualism and the most obvious one is you can communicate with people who speak more than one language.
2 And that's a very great advantage in the modern world in a number of different ways.
3 I think that's a very important point – you can understand other cultures better.
4 Yes, I think another key point here is self-confidence, actually.
5 I'm not sure why that is, but of course it's a big advantage.
6 Research shows that bilinguals are less likely to suffer from dementia in old age, so that's a long-term benefit, if you like.
7 So you could say that bilingual education provides a huge benefit for society in the long term.

b When we want to introduce important ideas in a discussion or presentation, we often use phrases with *adjective + noun*. For example:

	adj	nouns
a/the	main	point/benefit/advantage

In the table there are different adjectives. One is not correct for the noun. Which one do you think it is? Put a cross (✗) next to it.

adjectives	noun
1 central key large important	point
2 important certain significant major	advantage
3 high significant huge enormous	benefit

c Notice three different ways of using these expressions. The same word can go in the gap in each sentence. What is the word?

1 A key point is _____ bilingual people are often very creative.
2 Bilingual people are often very creative, so _____ is a significant benefit.
3 The fact _____ bilingual people are often very creative is a major advantage.

d Put the phrases in the correct order to make a sentence.

1 helps young people learn / a central / a good working memory / point is that
2 huge benefit / helps business is a / that bilingual education / the fact
3 in young people / important advantage / bilingual education / so that's an / builds self-confidence
4 the key point is / young people huge / bilingualism gives / opportunities in life
5 are usually better / speak two languages / cultures, so that's / people who / a significant benefit / at understanding other

STUDY SKILLS: UNDERSTANDING LECTURES AND PRESENTATIONS
The expressions in 3a are often used in academic discussions, presentations and lectures. How can they help you to understand?

4 PRONUNCIATION Stress

a ▶9.2 Listen to the sentences in 3a and look at the two words you underlined. Are both words stressed? Is one stressed more strongly than the other?

b Which of the rules about these words are true or false?

1 We often stress both the adjective and the noun.
2 The stress on the adjective is always weaker.
3 If we stress the adjective more, it emphasises the main point a bit more strongly.
4 If we stress the noun more, it shows we are less sure the information is a main point.
5 We can also stress adverbs like *very* that come before adjectives.

c ▶9.3 In these examples, the bold adjective is stressed more strongly. <u>Underline</u> the stressed syllable of the adjectives in bold.

1 The **central** point of his presentation was that learning a second language when you are young is easier.
2 Learning a second language also makes learning a third language easier, that's an **important** advantage.
3 A **significant** benefit of knowing two languages is that it can help you get a better job.
4 Living in a bilingual society is a **major** advantage if you want to learn another language.
5 An **enormous** benefit to knowing a second language is that it opens up a new world for you.

5 SPEAKING

a Choose one of the topics to talk about.

- the benefits of learning your first language
- the advantages of being able to speak English well
- the value of technology for second language learning
- the usefulness of independent study when you are learning a second language

b Make notes on your topic. Think of three main points and an explanation or example that supports the point. Use the table below.

Main point	Explanation / Example
learning German is an interesting cultural experience	you can read important literature in the original version

c 💬 Tell your partner about your topic. Use the expressions in 3a to make the important points clear. When you listen to your partner, note down the important points.

d What is an extra point that you can add to the ones your partner talked about?

1 SPEAKING

a 💬 Where do you prefer to buy things you need, at small shops or in large department stores or supermarkets? Why?

b Look at the pictures below. Which shows … ?

1 a shop assistant   2 a cashier   3 automated self-service

c 💬 Discuss the questions in pairs.

1 In your town or city do many shops have automated self-service?
2 If yes, do you prefer to pay this way or with a cashier? Why? If no, do they seem a good idea? Why / Why not?

2 VOCABULARY

a Match the words to the definitions.

1 ☐ retail   2 ☐ employ

a when you pay someone to do work for you
b when you sell things to people, usually in shops

b Match the **bold** words and phrases in 1–5 to definitions a–e.

1 ☐ Most successful **retailers** know that the customer is always right.
2 ☐ The **retail industry** makes billions of pounds every year.
3 ☐ He's currently **unemployed** and looking for a job.
4 ☐ The number of people **in employment** increased by 2% last year.
5 ☐ All the **employees** in the shop only work part-time.

a people who have got jobs
b the people who work for one particular business
c people who own shops and sell things
d when you don't have a job
e all businesses that sell products to people through shops or online

STUDY SKILLS: WORD FAMILIES

Notice in 2a and 2b how base words can make word families (e.g. *employ*: *(un)employment*, *employee*). This happens a lot with academic vocabulary. What can you do when you notice word families with new words?

THE ROLE OF SELF-SERVICE IN THE RETAIL INDUSTRY

In many shops and supermarkets these days, it is common to find self-service checkouts. This means the customer scans the product, puts it in a bag and then pays using a bank card or credit card. We call this automated customer service. In some shops, for example shops that sell electronic products, it's possible to find a robot giving a product demonstration. The robot can explain and show how a product works. [1]**A recent government report in the US has suggested** that about 45% of current jobs could be done by machine. Increased automated customer service will lead to changes in employment and the customer service experience.

[2]**According to** an investment company report, up to 7.5 million people who work in the retail industry in the USA could lose their jobs in the next few years. For example, in supermarkets, there are often 10 to 15 people who work as cashiers. With self-service checkouts, there only need to be two or three people who stand near the checkout to help customers if there are problems. Another example is the people who make sure there are enough products on supermarket shelves. Most of this work can be done by computers and machines. [3]**Most retailers believe** this is a positive thing because they can cut the cost of staff and this results in lower prices for customers. However, it clearly means more people will be unemployed and high unemployment has a very negative effect on society as a whole.

On the other hand, [4]**in the opinion of** some retailers, there will always be work for shop assistants. Self-service checkouts are efficient, but it means that customers and shop assistants have very few opportunities to talk to each other. When customers are buying products, they often want to talk to someone and ask questions about the product. [5]**The results of a bank survey have shown** that their customers prefer to talk to financial advisors. Robots can do some of that work and are very good at giving detailed information about products, but they probably are not so good at making a real human connection with customers.

In summary, it's better to have a balance between automated and personalised customer service. Machines are much more efficient and customers do not have to wait in a long queue to pay for something. If machines replace cashiers, then people who work in shops might have more time to talk to customers. This should mean shop assistants can really understand customer needs. Obviously, this will not happen if retailers make most of their staff unemployed. They need to make sure they employ enough staff to give their customers a good retail experience.

3 READING

a Read the student essay on page 29 about automated self-service in the retail industry. One of the five main points below is <u>not</u> in the essay. Read the essay quickly and find the point that is not included.

1 More automated self-service will mean change for customers and employees.
2 Automated self-service means fewer shop assistants and this makes prices cheaper.
3 Employees wages have dropped since self-service machines were introduced.
4 Shop assistants play a useful role in the retail industry.
5 Both machines and real shop assistants are necessary to make the retail industry successful.

b Read paragraphs 1–3 again. Underline evidence (some facts or research) that supports the main idea in each paragraph.

c Read paragraph 4 again.

1 What are positive points about self-service machines?
2 What are positive points about shop assistants?

d 🧠 CRITICAL THINKING
PREDICTING PROBLEMS

In paragraph 3, there is an example of a problem with having more automated self-service. What are other possible problems? Think about:

• customers' ability to use machines
• shop security
• problems with the machines

4 LANGUAGE FOCUS
Reporting facts and opinions

a Notice the expressions in bold in the text. Why does the writer use them? Choose the best answer.

1 to introduce her own opinions about the topic
2 to introduce information and points of view she has read about
3 to compare facts and opinions she has read about

b Sort the expressions into two groups.

Group A: subject & verb	Group B: phrases with no verb
1) A recent government report in the US has suggested …	2) According to …

c Answer the questions.

1 Which expressions introduce some kind of research?
2 Which introduce what other people think?
3 Why is the present perfect used in two of the expressions?

d Complete the paragraph with words and expressions from the box. When you use a verb, think about the correct tense. More than one answer is possible for some gaps.

suggest	according to	in the opinion of
show	believe	

One of the unexpected results of automated self-service is an increase in stealing from shops. A survey of British supermarkets [1] _____ that 1.6 billion pounds of products were stolen in a year. They [2] _____ that most of this stealing was done by people using self-service checkouts. [3] _____ the police, there are more stolen products that are being sold online and they [4] _____ it is becoming easier for people to steal things from supermarkets and department stores because of self-service. [5] _____ the retailers' association, shop owners and managers need to remember that shop assistants are often very good at noticing if a customer is stealing.

5 WRITING

a Plan an introduction to an essay on automated call centres. Use the notes below. Put them in a logical order. The first point is number 4 and the last one is number 2.

1 ☐ can use chatbots – get suggestions for product and order
2 ☐7 automated call centres – people who work in call centres lose jobs
3 ☐ recent research – large number of calls to bank – lost cards or forgotten PIN numbers
4 ☐1 many people phone call centres about very simple questions
5 ☐ experts – chatbots – the future
6 ☐ now technology can deal with these simple enquiries – companies don't need many call centre operators
7 ☐ chatbots = voice robots – answer text messages

b Work alone. Write the introduction. Use some of the expressions from 4b.

c 💬 Work in pairs and compare your introductions. How similar are they?

6 READING EXTENSION

a Read an online magazine article about automation in the retail industry. Choose the correct words to complete the sentences.

1 In the baker's shop, cakes and bread are made by *bakers / machines*.
2 In the electrical shop, *a robot is / the shop assistants are* showing customers a new product.
3 *People who study retail / Shop assistants* believe millions of employees will lose their jobs in the future.
4 *Governments / Retailers* know that personal contact with customers is always useful.
5 It *will / won't* always be difficult to have self-service checkouts when you buy a lot of things.
6 *Robots / Shop assistants* are the most efficient way of replacing products that have been sold.

b Read again and answer the questions.

1 Have you experienced either of the two examples described at the beginning of the article?
2 This article talks mostly about the UK. Is the situation the same in your country?
3 What new way of paying is talked about in the article?
4 What do you think is the future of the retail industry in your country?

AUTOMATION IN RETAIL: WHAT DOES THE FUTURE LOOK LIKE?

In a busy baker's shop in south east London, a customer is trying to decide between a piece of cake or a doughnut. These products weren't made by bakers – they were made by machines. Also, there is only one employee in the shop, but there are four checkouts. Once the customer has decided what she wants, she can scan the product herself and enjoy her cake or doughnut.

In an electrical shop in France, a robot is in the middle of a demonstration of the latest products from Samsung. Next to him are two sales assistants who are making sure that the robot is working properly. In a couple of years, maybe only one sales assistant will be required to keep an eye on the robot.

These are two examples of the effect that automation is having on the retail industry. Industry experts believe that very soon huge numbers of employees with lose their jobs as technology replaces them. In the next 20 years, as many as 2.1 million jobs could disappear from UK shops.

While governments increase the amount of minimum wages in different countries, retailers are trying to save money by cutting the number of staff they employ. Technology is helping them do this. However, they also realise that human contact is important in retail. This means they are unsure what the future of their industry will look like.

Some retailers suggest that there will always be a need for cashiers and shop assistants. Take the example of supermarkets. Self-service checkouts work well when you buy a small number of products. However, if you are buying food for a whole week, it is much easier to go to a cashier to pay for your shopping. Cashiers are often much faster at scanning products.

But there are new technological advances that could make even more changes. RFID stands for 'radio-frequency identification'. Each product will have an RFID label. This only needs to be pushed near a sensor – it doesn't need to be scanned. RFID can add up a week of food shopping in two or three seconds. It's very fast and efficient.

It is in the back of shops – the place a customer never sees – that technology is most useful. Robots can be used to check how many products are left and send an immediate request for replacements which are put on the shop shelves for customers. They can do all this in seconds.

Will robots and machines replace humans in retail? No-one wants to make a prediction, but for those people who work in this industry the future is not looking very safe.

Unit 11 Coffee

ACADEMIC SKILLS PLUS

Biology/Environmental studies: Recycling coffee grounds

Listening skills: Listening for main ideas and details; Recognising problem-solution patterns
Speaking skills: Providing supporting detail in presentations

1 SPEAKING

a 💬 Discuss the questions.

1 How much coffee do you drink each day?
2 What kind of coffee do you like to drink? For example, instant, espresso, cappuccino.
   OR
   Why don't you like drinking coffee?
3 Why do you think American-style coffee bars are popular? What do you think about them?

2 VOCABULARY Compound words and phrases

a Add words from the box to 1–7 to make new words or phrases.

fuel   fill   operation   grounds
waste   resource   beans

1 ☐ coffee _____
2 ☐ chemical _____
3 ☐ soya _____
4 ☐ land _____
5 ☐ bio _____
6 ☐ natural _____
7 ☐ commercial _____

b Match the words and phrases in 2a with definitions a–g.

a the place where the rubbish of a town or city is put in the ground
b small beans with a light colour – used to make different foods and drinks, for example, milk or yogurt
c the coffee that is left after making espresso coffee
d something from nature that is useful or valuable
e chemicals that are not useful and are like a kind of rubbish – bad for the environment
f an activity that can become a business and make a profit
g fuel that is made from living things and doesn't hurt the environment

c Complete the gaps with the words or phrases from 2a.

1 I can't drink cow's milk so I put milk made from _____ in my coffee.
2 In my part of the country there's a lot of wind so we use it as a _____ to create electricity.
3 When people throw away old medicine it can create _____ that is bad for the environment.
4 I drink a lot of coffee and keep the _____ to put on the garden – they're good for plants!
5 They started by making pasta sauce and selling it at a local market. It was very popular and now their business is a large _____ that earns over a million pounds a year.
6 The city doesn't recycle glass or plastic – they just put all the rubbish in a _____ site.
7 It seems crazy to think you can drive a car using plants, but _____ is becoming more commonly used.

3 LISTENING

a You will hear Sonia give a short presentation on coffee. She talks about three main problems:

1 using coffee grounds
2 the oil in coffee
3 producing biofuels

▶11.1 Listen and make notes about each problem.

b ▶11.1 Listen again. Sonia talks about the points below. Listen for more detail and add information to the notes.

1 Gardens: coffee grounds good _____
2 Engineers at Lancaster University: discovered new process to get oil from coffee grounds – faster _____
3 Oil from coffee can be used for _____
4 Landfills in the UK: _____ tonnes of coffee grounds / year
5 Benefits of coffee biofuel: natural resources not used; low _____; no need to _____

c 🧠 CRITICAL THINKING
ANALYSING PATTERNS / PROBLEM-SOLUTION

Use the information from 3a and 3b to complete this summary of Sonia's presentation.

Main problem: _____
Solution: _____
Evaluation of solution: _____

4 PRONUNCIATION Listening for small words

a Read the excerpt from the presentation. The words *the* and *that('s)* are left out. Can you predict where they go?

When you think about all coffee people drink around the world, do you ever stop to think about what happens to coffee left over – what we call coffee grounds?

b ▶11.2 Listen and check your predictions.

c In the excerpt below *the* and *a* are left out. Predict where they go.

You see, coffee grounds contain little bit of oil, but normally it's quite complicated process to get oil out of coffee.

d ▶11.3 Listen and check your answers.

e Match the missing words from 4a and 4c with the grammar terms.

1 ☐ the   a indefinite article
2 ☐ that   b definite article
3 ☐ a   c relative pronoun

f Answer the questions.

1 Is the pronunciation of these words in continuous speech usually weak or strong?
2 Do you need to understand these words to understand what someone is saying?

5 LANGUAGE FOCUS Adding information

a Read the examples from the presentation. Complete the sentences with the words and expressions in the box.

in addition   what's more   also   and as well as that

1 The coffee grounds need to be cooked at about 60 degrees for one or two hours and you need to add some chemicals to get the process started. _____, this means you get some chemical waste at the end of the process.
2 So this process is faster _____ it uses far less energy, which of course makes it much less expensive.
3 So producing biofuel from coffee grounds means using fewer natural resources. _____, it's a very low energy way of producing fuel. It _____ means we don't need to put more rubbish in landfills.

▶11.4 Listen and check your answers.

b Why do we use these words and expressions? Choose the best answer.

1 To compare the next idea with the one before
2 To make an extra point about an idea
3 To introduce the result of an idea that has been presented

c Answer the questions.

1 Which two expressions can be used in the same way?
2 In example 2, is it possible to take away 'as well as that'? Why do we use this expression?
3 In the second example in number 3, can 'also' go in a different place in the sentence?

d Cover 5a and 5c. Complete the Fact box below with the correct word(s).

Fact box:

Coffee drinking in the UK

1 In the UK, people are drinking more coffee and as _____ they are drinking less instant coffee and more better quality coffee.
2 Coffee shops have become very popular places for people to meet friends for a coffee. _____ more, people who go to these shops often buy good quality coffee beans to make their own special coffees at home.
3 In the UK, younger people think that coffee is a cool drink. They _____ think that tea, the traditional English drink, is a bit old-fashioned.
4 People drink their coffee in many different ways and they prefer an espresso or a cappuccino to instant coffee. In _____, they are changing their tea drinking habits because people are drinking more green tea or herbal tea and not the usual black tea.

e 💬 Think about people's drinking habits in your country. How have they changed? Write one or two sentences. Use an expression from 5a. Share your sentence(s) with other students.

6 SPEAKING

a Choose one of the topics below that you know something about. You will give a short presentation to another student about this topic.

- changes to food habits in your country
- a new process or invention that is good for the environment
- a new way to help people get fit
- a new discovery or research that helps people with health problems

b Think of three main points about your topic. For each main point think of an extra idea that adds interesting or useful information. Use the table to make notes.

Point	Main idea	Extra idea
1		
2		
3		

STUDY SKILLS: PLANNING PRESENTATIONS

You can use something similar to the table above when you plan presentations. How will it help you?

c 💬 Work in pairs. Give your short presentations to each other.

- use words and phrases from 5a
- listen to your partner, make notes on the main and extra ideas they give during the presentation
- read out your notes and check with your partner that you understood the main ideas.

ACADEMIC SKILLS PLUS

Sociology: Cultural studies

Reading skills: Understanding factual detail
Writing skills: Reporting statistical data;
Writing from notes

1 SPEAKING

a 💬 Discuss the questions.

1 Where do you live?
- at home with your parents
- in a flat (alone or shared with other people)
- in student accommodation
- in someone else's home

2 In your country, is this the same for most people of your age?

3 Would you prefer to live somewhere else if you had the choice? Why / Why not? If yes, where?

b 💬 Cover the text. Choose the correct answers to complete the gaps in the information about European countries. Discuss your ideas in pairs.

1 In Europe, _____ of people aged 18–29 live at home with their parents.
a 15%   b 30%   c 50%

2 The number of people in their 20s living at home is _____.
a increasing   b staying the same
c decreasing

3 The main reason people in their 20s live at home with their parents is _____.
a they can't afford to move away   b it's less trouble
c they're scared to move away

4 On average, children stay in their parents' home longer in _____.
a northern Europe   b western Europe
c southern and eastern Europe

5 On average, men move out of their parents' home _____ women.
a earlier than   b later than   c at the same age as

2 READING

30 and living with mum and dad

Is the idea of growing up and leaving home becoming a thing of the past? Yes, it is, according to the latest research.

Recent surveys have shown that there is a new generation of young adults in Europe who are growing up at home and not moving out. One in four people in Britain between the ages of 18 and 29 still lives at home with their parents, and the average over the whole of Europe is about twice as many. Almost half of Greek and Spanish people in this age group live with their parents, while 64% of Polish adults under 30 are still at home and nearly 70% of Italians.

There has been a steady increase in the number of adults in their 20s living with their parents – it has risen by over a quarter over the last two decades and is now at its highest point since records began in 1996. The phenomenon has become so normal over the last decade that people have given it a name – the 'Boomerang Generation', so called because typically children leave home to go to university and perhaps live alone for a time but then return to their parents' home.

Interviews with under-30s suggest that this growing trend to stay in the parents' home is not a result of laziness or lack of independence but is mainly economic. In EU countries, average youth unemployment is 25%, and the proportion is closer to

50% in countries such as Greece and Spain. Another factor is the cost of education: more and more young people are going to university and tuition fees are higher now than they were in the 1990s. In addition, property prices have risen across Europe and the cost of renting a flat in some cities is twice or three times as high as it was two decades ago.

However, cultural factors, such as the way families traditionally live together, also play a part. In Italy, for example, it's normal for several generations of a family to live together and children – especially sons – tend to stay at home until they marry. This may explain why there is a noticeable difference in the age at which children leave home in northern and western European countries and in southern and eastern European countries. In Sweden and Finland, for example, young people leave home on average before the age of 23, whereas in Spain and Greece the average age is above 28 and in Italy and Croatia it is around 30. In all countries, men stay in their parents' home longer than women, but the difference is greater in southern and eastern Europe. In Italy, for example, 73% of men aged 25–30 are still living in their parents' home.

a Read the article on page 34 and check your answers to the questions in 1b. Which answer … ?

1 did you guess most easily
2 did you find most surprising

b Read the article again and make brief notes on the topics below.

1 the 'boomerang generation'
2 factors which encourage people to live in their parents' home
3 cultural differences between southern and northern Europe

💬 Compare your notes with another student. Do you have the same points?

c Skills focus Understanding factual detail

Are these statements true (T) or false (F) according to the article, or don't we know (DK)?

1 Young people leave home later in Poland than they do in Sweden. _____
2 In 1996, most British people in their late 20s were still living at home. _____
3 It's difficult for young people to find a job in Spain – harder than in most other European countries. _____
4 About 70% of Italian men stay at home until they get married. _____
5 Most women in Sweden have left home by the time they're 25. _____
6 In Croatia, most men in their 30s are still living at home with their parents. _____

STUDY SKILLS: READING FOR DETAIL

How did you check the facts in 2c? Did you … ?

a read quickly through the article

b quickly find the right place in the article, then read that sentence carefully

c read slowly through the whole article from the beginning

Why is one of these ways of reading for detail better than the others?

---

3 VOCABULARY Words to describe trends

a Look at the phrases in bold.

1 ☐ Students **tend to** prefer sharing a flat, rather than living alone.
2 ☐ A high **proportion of** young people are taking low-paid jobs.
3 ☐ **One factor in** this is youth unemployment
4 ☐ There's **a growing trend** for people to take a year off before university.
5 ☐ **On average**, women in Europe leave home earlier than men.

Which phrase means …?

a more and more people are doing it
b the number compared with the total
c normally (it's true of most people)
d it has an effect on the situation
e it often happens

b Notice how the phrases in 3a are used in the article. According to the article …

1 What do children in Italian families *tend to* do?
2 What *proportion* is close to 50%?
3 What is *another factor* in people staying at home?
4 What *growing trend* is happening?
5 What do young people in Sweden and Finland do *on average*?

c 🧠 CRITICAL THINKING
GOING BEYOND THE FACTS

What are the positive and negative aspects of grown-up children staying at home with their parents? Make two lists:

Positive aspects	Negative aspects
For the children:	For the children:
_____	_____
For the parents:	For the parents:
_____	_____

Compare your answers. Did you find more positive or more negative aspects?

4 LANGUAGE FOCUS Proportions

a Cover the text. Complete the sentences with phrases that mean the same as the numbers in brackets.

one in four	twice as many	over a quarter
almost half	three times as	

1 _____ people in Britain between the ages of 18 and 29 still lives at home with their parents. (25%)
2 _____ of Greek and Spanish people in this age group live with their parents. (45–50%)
3 It has risen by _____ over the last two decades. (25%+)
4 The average over the whole of Europe is about _____. (x 2)
5 The cost of renting a flat in some cities is twice or _____ high as it was two decades ago. (x 3)

Read the text to check your answers.

STUDENT HOUSES TO LET
Tel: 01904 673399
Mob: 07808 929557
YorkStudentAccommodation.co.uk

b <u>Underline</u> the correct word to complete the sentences.

1 We use **of** *before* / *after* (a) half, a quarter, a third, etc.
2 We use **as** *before* / *after* twice, three times, four times, etc.
3 We use **by** *before* / *after* a half, a quarter, a third, etc
4 Another way to say **a quarter** is **one** *in* / *by* **four**.

c Write sentences based on the notes, using phrases from 4a. More than one answer may be possible.

1 *People who own a mobile phone: 30% of the world's population.*
2 *Unemployment: 2010 – 1 million, now – 1.5 million*
3 *People travelling abroad every year: 2000 – 30 million, now – 90 million*
4 *Young people at university: 24%*
5 *Average income: 10 years ago – $20,000, now – $22,000*

5 WRITING

a Look at the notes below 5d, which show data about numbers of children in European households. Do the notes give information about these topics? Write *Yes* or *No*.

1 average numbers for Europe _____
2 different kinds of families _____
3 numbers of boys or girls _____
4 ages of parents and children _____
5 changes over a decade _____
6 differences between countries _____

b 💬 Work in pairs. Discuss how you could describe some of the numbers in the notes using phrases from 4a.

- half / a quarter / a third of ...
- twice / three times as many as ...
- 1 in 4 / 1 in 10, ...
- increase/decrease by a quarter / by 2%, ...

c Write a paragraph, using the notes in 5a.

1 Think of an interesting general sentence to begin the paragraph.
2 Describe the data, using complete sentences.

d 💬 Compare your paragraph with another student. Did you describe the data in the same way?

- average households in EU countries – 31% have children
- 20% = couples with children, 25% = couples without children
- 2005–2015 households with children decreased (2005 – 33%, 2015 – 31%)
- families with children: Ireland – highest in EU = 42%; Germany – lowest = 21%

6 READING EXTENSION

a Read the article, which describes research about children who leave home late in life. Which of the ideas (a–e) below are … ?

1 results shown by the study
2 the author's own opinion
3 opinions the author doesn't agree with

a People who leave home early tend to live further away. _____
b There is something wrong with children who leave home later. _____
c Children who leave home later have a more loving relationship with their parents. _____
d Children who leave home later stay in touch more with their parents. _____
e It's a good idea for children to stay with their parents when they become adults. _____

b Complete the notes with words from the box.

babysitting	enjoy their life	35%
help the children		help the parents
in contact	31%	independent
more loving	more time	9%
other people	12%	

1 Possible problems if children stay in their parents' home too long:
   a They are different from _____.
   b They won't become _____.
   c Their parents won't be able to _____.
2 Three questions the survey asked:
   a How many days in the last year were the children _____?
   b Did the children _____ with jobs in the home?
   c Did the parents _____ with jobs in the home and _____?
3 Results:
   a Contact: Children who left home later spent _____ with their parents.
   b Helping parents: _____ of late leavers helped; _____ of early leavers helped
   c Helping children: _____ of late leavers received help from parents; _____ of early leavers received help.
4 Conclusion:
   Perhaps children who leave home late have a _____ relationship with their parents.

c Think about the writer's conclusion.

1 *Do you agree with it? Why? / Why not?*
2 *Think about your own family and other families you know. Do you think what the writer says is true about them?*

Mum or best friend?

The sooner you leave home, the further away you go. This is the clear conclusion from a recent survey of children leaving home. But what about other kinds of closeness between children and their parents?

People have believed for a long time that young adults who stay with their parents 'too long' are likely to have problems and cause problems for other people. First, they are not doing what everyone else is doing, at the same time as everyone else. They are 'failing' to become a real independent adult. They are a burden on their parents, preventing their parents from enjoying their time together.

But a recent study of nearly 15,000 parents and their grown-up children from 15 countries is more optimistic. It shows that when grown children live with their parents longer, they will have closer relationships later on.

The author of the study, Thomas Leopold, asked how many days of the last year the parents and their grown children were in touch with each other, either face-to-face or in some other way such as phone or mail. Here's what he found: the adult children who left their parents' home later also kept in touch better with their parents five years (or more) later. The latest to leave were in contact with their parents an average of 21 more days than those who left earliest.

He also asked these questions:

1 Did the grown children, in the past year, help their parents with home repairs, gardening, shopping, paperwork, or household chores?

2 Did the parents help their grown children with any of the above tasks, or with babysitting for the grandchildren?

The results showed a similar trend. Only nine per cent of those who left their parents' home early or at the usual time had helped their parents in the previous year. For those who were late to leave, 12 per cent helped their parents.

In turn, the late leavers also received more help from their parents than did those who left home at an earlier age (about 35 per cent compared to about 31 per cent Leopold says that a lot of that help was babysitting for the grandchildren.

In summary, the children who left home later were more often in touch with their parents after they had left. They also helped their parents a bit more often than did those who left earlier and their parents helped them a bit more, too.

Could it be that the parents and their children who live together a long time develop a more loving relationship? I think what may happen as children grow older is that the relationship between them and their parents becomes more like a friendship and less like a parent-child relationship. The relationship becomes more like equals. This may also happen when adult children return to live with their parents, and this must be good both for the parents and for the children.

1 SPEAKING

a 🗨 Read the quiz questions. Answer the questions with a partner.

QUIZ:
How do we really communicate?

True or false?

1. We understand 70% of a conversation from words. _____

2. We understand 25% of a conversation from a person's voice. _____

3. We understand 5% of a conversation from people's faces and bodies. _____

4. We use about 250,000 different facial expressions when we talk. _____

2 VOCABULARY

a Look at the photographs of types of body language. Match descriptions (1–6) with photographs (a–f).

1. ☐ blinking
2. ☐ mirroring
3. ☐ showing the palms of your hands
4. ☐ crossing your arms
5. ☐ flaring your nostrils
6. ☐ pointing

3 READING

a Read the first paragraph of the magazine article about body language on page 39. Were your answers to 1a correct? What information surprises you the most?

BETTER READING:
UNDERSTANDING WORDS FROM CONTEXT

You can sometimes guess the meaning of unknown words in a text from the context. Read the other words in the sentence before and after the new word. There are often clues to help you understand.

Look at the phrase from Section 1 of the article on page 39. If you show the <u>palms</u> of your hands, …

1. What are palms?
2. What other words in the sentence helped you understand? Underline them.
3. Read the rest of the article and guess the meaning of these words. Then check in a dictionary or with your teacher.
   - facial
   - flare
   - crossed

b 🗨 Work in pairs. Look at photographs a–f again. What does the body language mean, according to the article? Is this the same in your country?

c Read the article again. Answer the questions.

1. Why does Patricia say that the face is more important than words?
2. Which three types of body language help to create good relationships?
3. Which two types of body language can be viewed as aggressive?
4. When you 'mirror' someone, should you do exactly what they do? Why/Why not?
5. Which type of body language can have a negative effect on memory?

Home   **Business**   Politics   World   Technology

Don't Blink!
Body Language in the Business World

How do we understand someone in a conversation? People think we listen to language, but only 7% of communication comes from words. In fact, 55% of the information we receive is visual – it comes from the person's face and body. Some experts believe there are about 250,000 different facial expressions. Less information comes from the speaker's tone of voice – 38%. We also talk with our hands and feet, and even with our arms and legs.

Body language expert Patricia Hive says, 'In the business world, it's very simple. Success depends on body language. And it is especially important in business meetings and job interviews, because everyone is watching everyone else.'

So, what is the right thing to do? And what shouldn't you do? Here are Patricia's top suggestions.

1 The hands

Your hands are very important in meetings and interviews. If you show the palms of your hands, people think that you are interested in what they are saying – and you also appear open to their ideas. If you don't show your palms, they may think that you're not interested. It's also important not to point at people you are talking to. It can mean you want an argument or that you are competitive.

In their book, *The Definitive Book of Body Language*, Barbara and Allan Pease describe their university research. In one experiment, a lecturer gave exactly the same lecture to different groups of students. With the first group, the lecturer showed the palms of her hands a lot, and 84% of students said afterwards they thought the lecture was 'positive'. With the second group, she didn't show the palms of her hands, and only 54% of students said the lecture was 'positive'. When the same lecturer pointed a lot with a third group, only 28% said the lecture was 'positive'.

2 The face

Patricia says, 'The face says more than words. In a business meeting or job interview, people watch the face more than any other part of the body. It's important to remember that. Each small facial expression can mean something.' You should make eye contact because this means you're listening. But you shouldn't make too much eye contact. People might think you are angry or unhappy. Try not to blink too much either. People may think you're nervous or stressed. Some people also believe it means you're not being honest. There are other things to avoid. For example, if you flare your nostrils, people think you are angry or annoyed – so even your nose can send negative signals!

'The face is different for men and women,' Patricia says. 'Women show their emotions through their faces more. They can use six different facial expressions during ten seconds of conversation, while men can use just two. Women generally smile more than men too.'

3 Mirroring

When you're talking to someone in a meeting or interview, are they doing the same things as you? Do they smile when you do? Do they lean forward when you do? This is called 'mirroring', and it shows that the person likes you, or agrees with you. It's a good idea to try to mirror other people a little in meetings and interviews. But don't do it too much! First, watch the person's facial expressions and body language, and then start to do the same. This can help to get on together and create a good atmosphere in the room.

4 Body language and memory

Finally, your body language can help your memory. *The Definitive Book of Body Language* describes an experiment at a university. Two groups of students attended the same lecture. In the first group, the students crossed their arms and crossed their legs. In the second, they didn't. Both groups were tested on what they remembered from the lecture. The second group remembered 38% more than the first!

Patricia says, 'Remember every country is different. My suggestions work in the USA. But the rules are different in other countries.'

---

4 SPEAKING

a Work in pairs. Answer the questions with a partner.

1 Which suggestions in the article do you think are useful? Why?
2 Patricia's suggestions work in the USA, but the rules are different in other countries. Do her suggestions work in your country, or other countries you know? Why / Why not?
3 Make a list of three or four other examples of body language you know. Do you and your partner agree about what they mean?
4 What body language do you think you use a lot?

1 SPEAKING

a 💬 Work in pairs. Answer the questions.

1 When was your last holiday?
2 Where did you go?
3 What did you do there?

b 💬 Work in pairs. Ask and answer the quiz questions.

Quiz: What's your holiday personality?

When you go on holiday, do you usually …

1 a ☐ stay in your own country or   b ☐ go abroad?
2 a ☐ stay in a resort with other tourists or   b ☐ in a place near local people?
3 a ☐ eat food you normally eat or   b ☐ eat the local food?
4 a ☐ speak your own language or   b ☐ try to speak the country's language?

If you got more As, you don't like holiday adventures. If you got more Bs, you do!

2 VOCABULARY

a Match the words (1–5) with definitions (a–e). Compare your answers with a partner. Check in a dictionary.

1 ☐ flight   a visiting places of interest while on holiday
2 ☐ unpack   b an exchange, when someone gives something and gets another thing
3 ☐ swap   c a place where people on holiday can put a tent
4 ☐ sightseeing   d a journey by aeroplane
5 ☐ campsite   e to take things out of a suitcase or bag

3 READING

BETTER READING: PREDICTION

Reading the title of a text first helps you to understand the main idea. In a discussion forum, reading the first post also helps you to predict what kind of information will be in the text. This can help you understand the general topic of the discussion.

Read the title and the first post of the discussion forum below. Work in pairs and answer the questions.
1 What will the discussion forum be about?
2 How many suggestions can you think of for Nadia?

a Read the rest of the discussion forum and answer the questions.
1 Were your predictions correct?
2 Did you have the same idea as Juan?
3 Would you like to go on a holiday like this? Why / Why not?

b Read the discussion forum again. Answer the questions.
1 Why should you trust the people who stay in your home?
2 Why was Keira tired, stressed and nervous the first time?
3 What were the two problems Keira had before the woman answered the door?
4 Why was Keira worried when she stayed in Madrid?
5 What was positive about Keira's experience in Madrid?

4 SPEAKING

a You are going to swap your house with someone from another country.

Make notes about your home. It can be a real home or an imaginary one. Think about:

| city or countryside | number of rooms |
| garden/swimming pool | things to see and do |

b 💬 Work in groups. Ask and answer questions about your homes. Find someone to swap homes with. Agree on start and finish dates for the holiday.

Holiday Suggestions

Messages   Profile

Discussion forum

Nadia My family and I want to go on a really fun holiday for two weeks. But it also needs to be very cheap! Any ideas, anyone?

Juan Hi Nadia! We do a lot of home swap holidays. They're fantastic! You live in someone else's home during your holiday, and they stay in yours. You only pay for your flights so you can travel to lots of places. Actually, a man called Daniel Prince and his family have travelled non-stop around the world for over three years, using home swap stays!

Nadia That sounds amazing! But what's it like having strangers in your home?

Juan It was strange the first time, but now we find it normal. You should trust your visitors! Your visitors offer you their home in return, so they are trusting you, too.

Keira I agree with Juan. My family and I have had five great holidays in other people's homes. We stayed in Europe and Asia. We had one bad experience, but the rest were great.

I remember the first time we did it. My family and I were standing outside the front door of an apartment in Barcelona. That morning, our car broke down on the motorway, so we were tired and stressed. We were nervous, too – we saw lots of photos of the apartment before we left, but sometimes photos lie. Then my little boy lost his favourite toy, and he started screaming. I went back to the car to look for it, and unpacked all our bags. So my little boy was crying, and all our things were all over the pavement and suddenly a woman answered the door. She looked really nervous too! And then we all started laughing. It was a nice way to start!

Nadia That sounds like a stressful start to your holiday, Keira! I hope the rest of it was fun. What was the bad experience?

Keira Oh, it was last year. It was a bit of a nightmare! We were staying in a family's home in Madrid, and we woke up one morning, and there was water everywhere! It was coming through the ceiling. I tried to sort the problem out, but I couldn't. And my husband called the host family. He doesn't speak Spanish and they only speak a little English, so they didn't understand. He kept shouting: 'There is lots of water here!' I was really worried. We didn't have a phone number for a plumber in Spain either. Eventually, a neighbour came round. He found the source of the problem and stopped the water. He called a plumber and also called the family and explained everything. He helped us clean everything up. It was fine after that. He invited us round for dinner with his family, and we spent a lot of the holiday with them. We're still friends today, so there was an upside!

Nadia Oh, that sounds terrible! But do you still recommend home swap holidays?

Keira Oh, yes, definitely! Usually on holiday, you stay in a hostel, campsite or hotel and you go sightseeing with your guidebook. You spend most of the time with other tourists, and you speak your own language. But when you live in someone else's home, you live in their culture. You go to their supermarkets. You go to the same restaurants. Your neighbours are local people, not other tourists. You see how people really live in that country. I strongly recommend it.

Nadia OK, Keira. Thanks! I think we'll try it.

Juan And Nadia, don't forget – it's free!

1 SPEAKING

a 💬 Work in pairs. Answer the questions.

1 What are the advantages and disadvantages of borrowing money from these people or places?
   - friends
   - family
   - a bank
   - work

2 How much money would you feel comfortable borrowing from the people or places?

b 💬 Do you ever lend money to people? Why / Why not?

2 VOCABULARY

a Complete the table. Compare your answers with a partner. Check your answers in a dictionary.

verb	noun	person
		lender
borrow	–	
	bank	
		investor

3 READING

BETTER READING:
INTRODUCTORY PARAGRAPHS

Sometimes, the first paragraph can help you understand the topic of the whole text.

1 Read the introductory paragraph to the article on page 43. What do you think the article is about? Discuss your ideas with a partner.
2 Read the whole article. Were your ideas correct?

a Read the article again. In which text(s) (1–4) ... ?

1 did the same thing happen in two places
2 can you get a loan to start a business (x3)
3 do you ask lots of people for money to start a business (x2)
4 do you get a loan from a bank
5 does the idea help people in developing countries (x2)
6 do people ask for money for education

b Read the article again and answer the questions. Why did ... ?

1 Franz Hermann Schulze-Delitzsch start his credit union
2 Dr. Muhammad Yunus start his 'Village Bank'
3 the music group ask fans for money
4 Hans Fex ask for money

c Note down what these numbers in the article refer to.

1 25
2 100
3 26,000
4 1.2 million
5 8.81 million
6 1.02 billion

4 SPEAKING

a 💬 Work with a partner. Which idea (1–4) in the article do you like the most? Why?

b 💬 Work in groups of three or four. Choose a crowdfunding project from the table to lend money to.

Who are they?	They want money to ...	They offer ...
1 'The New Beats', a rock group	buy new musical instruments	free tickets to see the group for a year
2 Julia, an artist	do a show of her paintings in Sao Paolo	0.5% of profits for $1,000 loan
3 A group of local people	create a garden in a poor area of the city	your name will be on the wall in the garden
4 A woman in Kenya	start a basket making business	1% of profits for £100 loan

c 💬 Tell the class which project you chose. Explain why you chose it.

d 💬 Do you know any projects which need crowdfunding? Tell the class.

When the bank says 'NO!'

Have you ever tried to get a loan, but the bank said 'No!'? Maybe you can't afford a loan, or you don't have a bank account? People have got loans or borrowed money in different ways for hundreds of years, and not just from banks.

❶ Credit unions

In the 1850s, Franz Hermann Schulze-Delitzsch was fed up with banks. He wanted to help other people, and he created a new organisation. People paid a little money each month. If someone wanted to borrow money, they could. The idea was a big success. At around the same time, Ninomiya Sontoku did something similar in his village in Japan. Everyone in the village could borrow money for up to 100 days. If the person couldn't pay back the money, the whole village helped them to repay it.

❷ Microcredit

In the 1970s, there were lots of problems in Bangladesh. Many people in villages were poor and hungry, and they couldn't get loans from normal banks. Dr. Muhammad Yunus, a professor of economics, found an answer. He gave very small loans to people (for example, $25), and they started small businesses. For instance, they made furniture or bought animals for farming. Dr. Muhammad Yunus's 'Village Bank' was born. In 2006, Yunus won the Nobel Peace Prize for his work with the poor. In 2015, the bank had 8.81 million borrowers in 81,392 villages. 97% of their customers were women.

❸ Crowdfunding

In 2007, a London music group needed money to make an album. They asked their fans for help online. They said that if the fans gave them money, they could have some of the profits later on. They received £26,000 from a thousand fans! Since then, lots of bands have done the same. This is one example of crowdfunding. You ask lots of people to each give a small amount of money to help you to start a business. And if the business makes a profit, you give the people some of it. So they may get some of their money back or not. They could also make some profit!

People have tried to crowdfund lots of strange and interesting things. Hans Fex wanted money for his Mini Museum. He creates tiny 'museums' you can put in your pocket. The museums include rock from the moon, and pieces of dinosaur egg. He raised $1.2m from 5,030 people. He now has his own website and has created three different museums. The first two have sold out.

❹ Kiva.org

Kiva.org is a very special crowdfunding website. It is for poor people, or those in developing countries like India. Some of them want to start a business, and others need money to go to school or university.

The idea is very simple. A borrower asks for a loan. It is posted on the Kiva website. Then lenders can then choose to lend money to the borrower. The minimum loan is $25. The borrowers use the money and repay the loans. 97% of loans are repaid. The lenders can then take the money or invest it in someone else.

So far, Kiva has had 2.5 million borrowers in 83 countries. There have been 1.5 million lenders. They have lent 1.02 billion dollars. Oprah Winfrey said: 'Kiva is a simple concept that can change a person's life.'

1 SPEAKING

a 💬 Work in pairs and follow the instructions.

You are planning a day out with some friends from another country.

1 Think about a city that you know. It can be where you live or a different city.
2 Make a list of interesting places that tourists can visit.
3 Agree on two or three places you'd both like to go to.

2 VOCABULARY

a Read the blog on page 45 quickly and find the adjectives in the box below in the text. Match the words to the definitions (1–6).

```
spooky    magical    underground    tiny
frightening    thought-provoking
```

1 very small _____
2 makes you feel fear _____
3 makes you think a lot about something _____
4 having a very exciting or special quality _____
5 a place can be strange and scary. _____
6 below the surface _____

3 READING

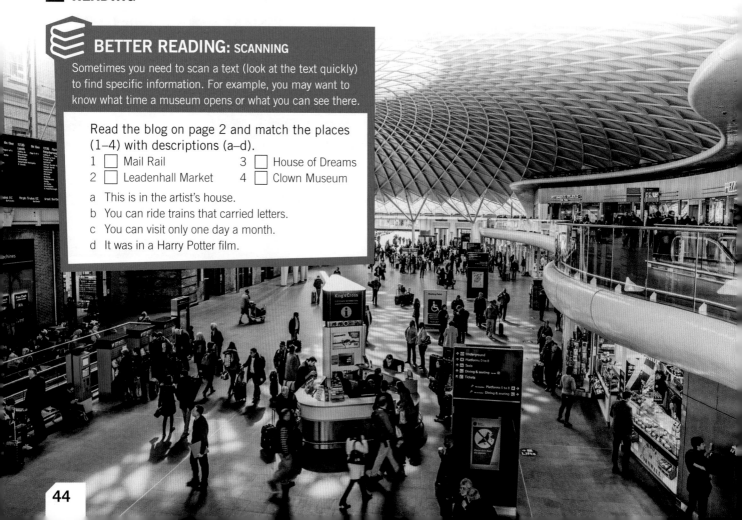

BETTER READING: SCANNING

Sometimes you need to scan a text (look at the text quickly) to find specific information. For example, you may want to know what time a museum opens or what you can see there.

Read the blog on page 2 and match the places (1–4) with descriptions (a–d).
1 ☐ Mail Rail   3 ☐ House of Dreams
2 ☐ Leadenhall Market 4 ☐ Clown Museum

a This is in the artist's house.
b You can ride trains that carried letters.
c You can visit only one day a month.
d It was in a Harry Potter film.

a Read the blog again and answer the questions. Write L (Leadenhall Market), M (Mail Rail), C (Clown Museum), P (Platform 9¾) or H (House of Dreams Museum).

Which place ... ?
1 has been used in films _____ _____
2 is the oldest _____
3 is not open at normal times _____ _____
4 is not where you think it is _____
5 is made out of things the artist has obtained _____

b Read the blog again. What are/were the following things used for?

1 the Mail Rail before it was open for tourists _____
2 Platform 9¾ in the Harry Potter film _____
3 the artist's house _____
4 the egg faces _____

4 SPEAKING

a 💬 Work in groups and discuss the questions.

1 Which place in the blog would you most like to visit? Why?
2 What are some alternative places for tourists to visit in your country? Tell each other about them. Which of your classmate's places would you most like to visit? Why?

Blog   Home   Followers   Share

London School of English **School Blog**

Cool London – The Other Side of the City

If you're going to a fun new place in London, and you'd like other students to come with you, post your ideas here.

Manuel – Mail Rail

I'm going to a really spooky place at the weekend, if anyone wants to come. I recently read that there's a secret railway under London, but no one knows about it. It is deeper underground than the famous Tube. The trains run on batteries and there are no drivers. I've posted a photo here. It was built 100 years ago by the Post Office, and it carried four million letters around London every day. But it was finally shut down in 2003. Now they've reopened the Mail Rail to the public, and you can go for a ride along the old tunnels. I think it will be really interesting. Do you think it will be frightening?

Anna and Kyoko – Film sets in London

Kyoko and I are going to do a little tour of London on Saturday. We're big Harry Potter fans, and we're going to visit a couple of places which are in the films.

First, we're going to Leadenhall Market, which has been there for over 600 years! It is really beautiful, and is a great place to buy flowers, cheese and meat. There's a place in Harry Potter and the Philosopher's Stone called Diagon Alley. Well, that's Leadenhall Market. Have a look at the photo. It really does look like a strange and magical place.

After that, we're going to King's Cross train station! That's where the student wizards in the Harry Potter films catch the train to go to Hogwarts School. In the film, they catch the train from a special platform called Platform 9¾. To get there, they have to walk through a wall between platforms 9 and 10! In reality, there's a train track between platforms 9 and 10, but there's a platform 9¾ on the station concourse. You can have your photo taken there. There's also a Harry Potter shop there.

So, we're meeting at the school at 11 a.m. on Saturday if anyone would like to come along.

Kim and Santiago – The House of Dreams Museum

We're going to the House of Dreams Museum, a little art gallery in South London. It's on a normal street, inside the artist's house.

He has turned his home and garden into a piece of art. And you can visit and walk around. Every surface of his house is covered in things he's found and arranged in interesting and thought-provoking ways. These include false teeth, children's toys, bottle tops and pen lids. I think it looks like one of the most colourful and magical places I've ever seen. You have to email him and book an appointment to see it. So, leave a comment below if you want to come and then I'll email him.

Kuba – Clown Museum

I'm planning to go to a clown museum on Friday after class if anyone's interested. It's tiny and you can only visit on the first Friday of the month. Britain has had many famous clowns and the museum displays lots of their costumes and props.

Guess what! There's a rule in the world of clowns – you can't have the same make-up as another clown. In the past, they painted their faces onto eggs, so no one would copy them. There are 200 of these eggs in the museum. I can't wait to see them!

1 SPEAKING

a 🗨 Work with a partner. Answer the questions together.

1 How many hours a week do people usually work in your country?
2 Has this changed in the last fifty years? Why / Why not?

2 READING 1

a Read the information about the average number of hours people work around the world in article 1 below. Answer the questions.

1 In which country do people work the longest hours?
2 Do people in France work more hours than people in Germany?
3 Do people work the same number of hours in Spain and Turkey?
4 Where do people work the fewest hours?

b 🗨 Work with a partner. Do you think people are happier if they work more, or less? Why?

Article 1

How many hours do people work around the world?

People in some countries are working very long hours. In Mexico, for example, people work 2,246 hours a year on average. But in other places people are working less than ever before. In France, there's a 35-hour working week. In Germany people work 1,371 hours a year. That's fewer than 30 hours a week.

Country	Hours worked per year	Country	Hours worked per year
Mexico	2,246	Japan	1,719
South Korea	2,113	Spain	1,691
Chile	1,988	UK	1,674
Turkey	1,832	Netherlands	1,419
Italy	1,725	Germany	1,371

Source: OECD: https://data.oecd.org/emp/hours-worked.htm

3 VOCABULARY

a Match the words (1–4) with definitions (a–d). Compare your answers with a partner. Check in a dictionary.

1 ☐ stressed
2 ☐ overtime
3 ☐ average
4 ☐ work-life balance

a time spent working compared with time spent doing things you enjoy
b working more time or later than is usual for a job
c nervous and worried
d a usual or typical level

4 READING 2

BETTER READING: TOPIC SENTENCES

The first sentence in each paragraph often gives a summary of what the paragraph is about. This is called the *topic sentence* and it can help you to predict what kind of information you will find in the rest of the paragraph.

1 Work in pairs. Read the first sentence of each paragraph in article 2 on page 47. Make a list of the ideas you think will be in each paragraph.
2 Read the article. Were you correct?

c Read article 2 again. In the writer's opinion, are these statements true or false?

1 Working less makes the writer's life better, but it won't make everyone's life better.
2 If you work more, you have more ideas.
3 If people work less, they sit on the sofa and watch more TV.
4 Working less can make us healthier.
5 If everyone works shorter hours, more people can work.
6 Shops and businesses are open in the evenings because people work long hours.
7 People in the 19ᵗʰ century thought it was impossible to work less.

d 🗨 Work in pairs. Read the comments section. Answer the questions with *A* (Alex), *L* (Laura) or *G* (Gabriela).

Who says that …?
1 it's important to like your job. _____
2 people don't work well when they work long hours. _____
3 hard work helps people become more confident. _____
4 working less can be good for your health. _____
5 having free time is less important than working. _____

Do you agree with any of the comments? Why?

Article 2

I have the answer to the world's problems: work less

Listen, I have a secret, the answer to all our problems: we need to work less. I know it seems crazy but I believe it will make the world a better place. Years ago, I used to work very long hours. I was doing about 15 hours overtime per week. Then I decided to work only four days a week. It changed my life. And I think it can change your life, too. Let me explain.

For a start, people do a better job if they work less. In one major study, workers produced more work if they worked fewer than 40 hours a week. When I worked long hours, I was always tired and I never had good ideas. I often made mistakes, too. If we all work long hours, we don't have time to spend with the people we love, our friends and families. We are also more stressed and we have less energy, so we often sit on the sofa and watch television at the end of the day, worrying about work. That can make us overweight and ill. Working fewer hours gives us more time to do other things outside work. We can do exercise, look after the family more and see our friends more often. This gives us a healthy work-life balance, which can then have a positive effect on our work. Also, if everyone works less, there will be more jobs for other people. More people will have more money to spend, so it's good for shops and businesses.

People also think it's impossible to work fewer hours because customers want more and more products. The point is we want too much. We want to go shopping in the evenings and we want things delivered to our homes at the weekends. Our shops and businesses are now often open 24 hours a day, seven days a week. How can this continue, people ask, if everyone is working less? Well, it can't continue. And that's a good thing.

There will always be people who disagree. They think that long hours and hard work are good for you, but I think this is really a 19th century idea. We only get one life. Personally, I don't want to spend it all working. I chose to work less and I've never been happier. Try it. It's the future!

Comments

 I disagree with the writer's opinion. Working hard is good for you! It makes you a better person. It makes you more confident, too. *Alexander, Russia*

 I think it would be a good idea to work less. When you work too many hours, you can't concentrate properly and your work is less efficient. If you don't have time to exercise each day, it's bad for your health, too, and that affects the quality of your work. *Laura, Spain*

 For me, work is more important than holidays and free time. You spend most of your life working. You have to enjoy it! I'm a doctor and I love it! *Gabriela, Brazil*

✂ Share 👍 Like 💬 Comment

5 SPEAKING

a 💬 Work in pairs. Answer the questions.

1 How many hours do you work a week? Would you like to work more or less? Why?
2 If you don't work, how many hours do you study each week? How does this compare with the average working week? Would you like to study more or less? Why?
3 Imagine you are in charge of your country. Decide on the number of:
   • hours people work a week   • weeks holiday a year   • public holidays a year

1 SPEAKING

a 💬 Look at the photos (a–e) of extreme sports and activities. Work in groups and answer the questions.

1 Have you or anyone you know ever done any of these things? How did you / they feel?
2 Why do people do sports and activities like this?
3 Why do people like doing frightening activities?

2 VOCABULARY

a Complete the definitions below with words from the box. Compare your answers with a partner.

fence	gap	breath	engine	controls

1 machine, part of a car that makes it move _____
2 a small space between two things _____
3 something people use to operate a machine or vehicle
   _____
4 a structure made of metal or wood to close a field or garden
   _____
5 the air that goes in or out of the mouth _____

3 READING

BETTER READING:
USING HEADINGS TO PREDICT CONTENT

Sometimes, before you read a text for the first time, it can help you understand better if you can predict what kind of information you'll find in the text.

The headings in the text *Days Out with a Difference*, on page 49, are questions.
1 Read only the questions in the text.
2 Talk about possible answers with a partner.
3 Read the text quickly. Were your guesses correct?

a Read the web page again. Answer the questions.

1 Which days out are dangerous?
2 In which day out does the instructor do something first, and then you do it?
3 In which days out does someone help you?
4 In which day out are there different ways of doing something?
5 How did Roberto, John and Kyoko feel when they did the activities?
6 How did the experience change Roberto, John and Kyoko?

a rollercoaster ride

a bungee jump

skydiving

abseiling

paintballing

Days Out
with a Difference.com

Are you tired of doing the same things? Do you like new and extreme experiences? Do you like being challenged or frightened? Then this is the website for you. Buy a day out for you, or as a gift for someone you know.
Click on an experience below to find out more.

Feed a big cat

How about feeding one of the world's biggest cats? By hand!

What happens on the day?

You will meet your zoo keeper and learn how to prepare the animal's food. They will then take you to the Lion or Tiger Enclosure. Don't worry! The lion or tiger will be on the other side of a very strong fence. You'll pass the meat through a gap in the fence, and the animal will take it from you.

What do customers say about it?

'It was frightening to be so close to the tiger. I had the meat in my hand and the tiger opened its mouth. I wanted to run away. It was huge! I could feel its breath on my face. My hand was shaking. My friend was so scared, he decided not to do it. But the zoo keeper was great. He explained what to do and I felt less frightened after a few minutes. The experience has made me much more interested in big cats, and in wild animals in general.'

Roberto, Ecuador

A flying lesson

Have you ever wanted to fly a plane? Well, now is your chance!

What happens on the day?

When you arrive, you will have a short lesson about the plane and general safety. Then you'll take off! The instructor will fly the plane for the first thirty minutes, and you can enjoy the amazing views of the countryside. Then it's your turn. You will fly the aeroplane for thirty minutes. But don't worry! Your instructor is there to take over if there's a problem!

What do customers say about it?

'Before we took off, I was just really excited. I've never been in a small plane before. The engine was really noisy, but the views were amazing. When it was my turn and I took over the controls, I was really frightened. The control panel looked more complicated than in a car. Then suddenly I was flying the plane! But it was fantastic. I felt like a bird – I was so free. I'm going to save some money and take more flying lessons next year.'

John, USA

Zorbing

Have you ever travelled in a large ball? When you go down a hill, you can go over 20mph!

What happens on the day?

When you arrive, you get inside the ball. It's completely safe. You then go down a big 160-metre hill. And at the end, you land in a pool with a big splash!

You can choose from two kinds of balls. There's normal zorbing, which is more comfortable, and then there's hydro-zorbing. Hydro-zorbing is a little different. We put 40 litres of water in the ball with you!

What do customers say about it?

'I was really frightened before I did it. But I absolutely loved it! I couldn't stop laughing. It was really strange to be inside a big ball. And I was surprised to go so fast. I did the hydro-zorbing – I felt as if I was inside a washing machine. I got very wet! But it was the best day out. The experience has made me more confident.'

Kyoko, Japan

4 SPEAKING

a Work individually. Which day out would you most like to do? Choose your favourite, your second favourite and least favourite.

b Work in pairs. Compare your ideas with a partner. Are your choices the same or different? Tell your partner why you made your choices.

1 SPEAKING

a Work in pairs. Discuss the questions.

1   Who do you think are generally the happiest people? Why?

babies   children   teenagers
middle-aged people   people over 60

2   When were you happiest in your life?

2 READING 1

a Read the quiz and answer the questions.

How much do you know about teenagers?

Look at the facts about teenagers. Choose the correct answer *a* or *b*.

1 Teenagers sleep _____ a night on average.
   a ☐ 6–8 hours   **b** ☐ 9–10 hours
2 Teenagers generally have _____ accidents than adults.
   a ☐ more   **b** ☐ fewer
3 Teenagers are often _____ than younger children.
   a ☐ more relaxed   **b** ☐ angrier
4 Teenagers understand other people's _____ better than children.
   a ☐ body language   **b** ☐ opinions
5 Teenagers stop _____ when they become adults.
   a ☐ living with their parents   **b** ☐ growing

b Read the article on page 51 about the teenage brain. How many of your answers in 2a were correct? Compare with a partner.

BETTER READING:
UNDERSTANDING WORDS FROM CONTEXT

Sometimes, you can understand an unknown word from the context. Look at the <u>underlined</u> words below from the text and answer the questions.

They walk off and <u>slam</u> doors.
Teenagers are often really <u>clumsy</u>.

1 What kind of word is it? (e.g. a verb, noun or adjective)
Look at the words before and after it (e.g. a noun sometimes follows *a/an*).
Look at the beginnings and endings of the words (e.g. a verb sometimes has an *ed* ending).

2 What's the topic or topics? (e.g. teenagers, the brain, growing up)

3 Which is the correct definition of 'slam'?
   a   *slam* (v) to close a door or window slowly and quietly
   b   *slam* (v) to close a door or window quickly and loudly

4 Which is the correct definition of 'clumsy'?
   a   *clumsy* (adj) to do something with little skill
   b   *clumsy* (adj) to do something with a lot of a skill

AMAZING FACTS ABOUT THE
TEENAGE BRAIN

The problem isn't teenagers – it's their brains. We know that being a teenager is the most difficult time in your life. It's also the most stressful time for parents! But don't blame the teenagers. Blame their brains.

Teenagers sleep a lot. They need about 9–10 hours' sleep a night, while adults need 6–8 hours. But they are not staying in bed because they are lazy. It's because the levels of the 'sleep' hormone, melatonin, increase in teenagers later at night than in children or adults, and these hormone levels decrease later in the morning for teenagers. That's why teenagers fall asleep later than adults, and wake up later.

Teenage boys have lots of little accidents. They drop things. They knock over cups of coffee. Teenagers are often really clumsy. This is because they are growing so quickly. Sometimes boys can grow 3 centimetres in 3 months. And when the body grows quickly, the brain doesn't know how to control it. It has to learn, and that takes time.

Teenagers do dangerous things. They go climbing, or they go swimming in dangerous water. This is because their brains are changing. The front part of the brain plans things. But in a teenager's brain, there are few connections between different parts of the brain. So, teenagers don't plan before they do something. They just do it. It's also because the 'pleasure centre' of the brain is very large when you're a teenager. That's why music sounds so great when you're 15. It also means you look for pleasure and enjoyment more, and that can be dangerous. But this pleasure centre can also be very positive for learning. A recent study at Leiden University in the Netherlands shows that teenagers are very sensitive to positive feedback in class. This means that the teenage years are the best time to acquire and process information.

Teenagers have lots of emotions. They shout, they cry. They walk off and slam doors. The problem is an important part of the brain called the *limbic system*. It creates memories and emotions, and it grows when you're a teenager. So teenagers are more likely to feel strong emotions. They are often angrier, or more frightened, than younger children.

Teenagers worry about people's opinions. They want to be cool. They want their friends to like them. When teenagers' brains grow, they develop new skills. They can understand other people's opinions better than younger children. They can see themselves from the viewpoint of others, especially their friends. And so the opinions of their friends become more important.

But the teenage years soon end, and you become an adult. You start to need less sleep. Your body stops growing, and your brain learns how to control it. The 'pleasure centre' becomes smaller when you're an adult too. And the front part of your brain is closely connected to the rest of it. And then you're an adult. And life becomes easier – and maybe a little more boring!

3 VOCABULARY

a Find the highlighted words in the article. Try to guess the meaning. Then match the words to the definitions (1–4).

1 A feeling of happiness or satisfaction: _____
2 To let something fall by mistake: _____
3 To get or obtain something: _____
4 A chemical produced by the body: _____

4 READING 2

c Read the article again. Are the statements true or false?

1 Teenagers sleep a lot because they are lazy.
2 Teenagers have lots of accidents because their brains are growing.
3 Teenagers do dangerous things because they can't plan.
4 Teenagers have lots of emotions because they have more memories.
5 The brain's pleasure centre makes teenagers enjoy music more than other age groups.
6 Teenagers worry about their friends' opinions because their friends have new skills.
7 Teenagers' brains change when they become adults.

5 SPEAKING

a Talk in groups. What information in the article surprised you? What information did you already know?

b What do you think are the biggest challenges for teenagers? Talk about some of these things or your own ideas.

- friends
- school
- exams
- parents
- emotions

c What age would you like to be now? Why?

2–5 years old	6–12 years old	13–17 years old
18–25 years old	25–35 years old	
35–45 years old	55–70 years old	

1 SPEAKING

a 💬 Ask and answer the questions with a partner.

> I prefer watching films at the cinema. It's a night out and it's more sociable.

> I like reading books on my e-reader. I have all my books in one place.

What's your favourite way to … ?
- watch films or TV series
- read books
- listen to music

Why do you prefer those ways?

2 VOCABULARY

a 💬 Which verbs from A do you associate with the nouns in B? How many verb + noun collocations can you make? Compare your ideas with a partner.

A	
listen (to)	stream
download	watch

B		
books	e-books	audiobooks
records	songs	music
videos	films	

b 💬 Use at least four of your collocations from 2a to discuss how you use technology with culture.

3 READING

a Look at the ideas from the article on page 53. Can you think of reasons for these things?

1 We listen to books nowadays, we don't read them.
2 People say the cinema is dying, but it isn't. It's changing.
3 We listen to songs nowadays, not albums.

b Read the article to check. Were your reasons correct?

c Read the article again and look at 1–9 below. Which are more popular now than before? Which are less popular than before?

1 books
2 e-books
3 audiobooks
4 films on phones and tablets
5 films at cinemas
6 films at luxury cinemas
7 albums
8 vinyl records
9 streamed songs

BETTER READING:
FINDING STATISTICS QUICKLY

It's important to be able to quickly identify statistics which support the writer's ideas or point of view.

> **1** Find statistics in the text to support ideas a–f below. Follow the steps in the box to help you.
>
> ---
>
> - scan the text (read quickly, without paying attention to every word) looking for numbers or key words (e.g. e-books, audiobooks, cinema).
> - find a number or key word.
> - read the sentence that contains the number or key word.
>
> ---
>
> a People are reading fewer e-books.
> b People are downloading more audiobooks.
> c People are going to the cinema less.
> d People are listening to more songs.
> e People are listening to fewer albums.
> f People are listening to more vinyl records.

d Complete the sentences with the statistics from the article.

1 Sales of e-books went down by _____ in the UK in 2016.
2 In 2015 downloads of audiobooks went up _____ .
3 _____ people went to the cinema in the USA and Canada in 2015.
4 People in the USA streamed _____ songs.
5 In the first half of 2016 _____ vinyl records were sold in the USA.

Technology and Culture

Technology has changed culture for many years. When the gramophone was invented, we could listen to albums in our own homes. After the camera was invented, we could take photographs and hang them on our walls. Now we have the Internet, smart phones and tablets, we can carry hundreds of albums and photographs with us at any time. And things are changing faster than ever. We invited three industry experts to talk about the future of culture.

'We listen to books nowadays, we don't read them.'
– Eduardo Pirlo, Head of Now Books

We are reading fewer books than ever before. The Pew Research Centre says that fewer books are read by older teenagers. Other research says books aren't read for fun anymore, and it's the same for adults. So why is this? When we read a book, we are not online so we feel disconnected from the world. We feel we are missing something. We don't have the latest news. We are not on social media, so we don't know what our friends are doing.

We are also reading fewer books on our screens. Sales of e-books fell 3% in 2016 in the UK. We look at our screens all the time, so perhaps people are tired of them.

We are listening to books more than we are reading them. Downloads of audiobooks increased by 38.1% in 2015. Perhaps that is because it's easier to listen than to read. And you can listen while you're doing other things, like driving.

'We listen to songs nowadays, not albums.'
– Bob Nichols, Head of DWR Music

The Internet has changed the music industry since the 1990s. We are buying fewer albums, but we are streaming more music. The Internet is killing the album. 209 billion songs were streamed in the USA in the first half of 2016. But only 100 million albums were bought during the same period. Perhaps people don't want to listen to a whole album by one artist any more. Maybe they only want to listen to the best songs.

And we don't only want to listen to music nowadays, we also want to watch something at the same time. In 2016, 46% of streamed songs were videos. We all love this new technology, but we also miss the nostalgia of the past. 6.2 million vinyl records were sold in the first half of 2016 in the USA. That's an increase of 11.4%!

'People say the cinema is dying, but it isn't. It's changing.'
– Jess Adams, ADF Films

In the past, we watched TV series in our living rooms and watched films at the cinema. But now we have smart phones and tablets. We can watch them at any time and any place. 4.4 billion people went to the cinema in the USA and Canada in 2006, but only 3.8 billion did the same in 2015. But cinemas aren't dying – they're changing to win audiences back. There are now more, smaller cinemas, and they offer more comfort and luxury. You can watch a film on a sofa or in an armchair. Waiters bring you food and drink! They're more expensive though!

4 SPEAKING

a 💬 Ask and answer the questions with a partner.

1 Do you agree with Eduardo Pirlo, Jess Adams and Bob Nichols? Why / Why not?
2 How much time do you spend doing these things?
   • reading books
   • reading things on social media
   • listening to audiobooks
   • listening to songs
   • listening to complete albums
   • watching films on your phone or tablet
   • watching films at the cinema
3 Imagine your perfect life. How much time would you like to spend doing these things?

1 SPEAKING

a Ask and answers the questions with a partner.

1 Can you remember your friends from your primary school? What were they like?
2 Do you know any of them now? What do they do?
3 What were you like at primary school?
4 When you were a child, what did you want to be when you grew up? Has that changed?

2 READING

BETTER READING:
SKIMMING TO IDENTIFY THE MAIN IDEA IN A TEXT

When you read, it isn't always necessary to understand every word – you just need to understand the main idea, or *gist*, of the text. This is called *skimming* – reading quickly to understand the main idea.

1 Skim blog post 1, *Class Reunion*, by a retired teacher called Sheila, below. Tick all the statements that apply to the text.

☐ Sheila isn't going to the class reunion.
☐ Sheila has very happy memories of teaching this class.
☐ Sheila's students had different ambitions for the future.

2 Compare your answers with a partner.

a Read blog post 1 again and answer the questions.

1 How does Sheila feel about the reunion?
2 How does Sheila feel about her old class?
3 What three things did she find recently?
4 Which ambition do you like the most or the least? Why?

Blog post 1

Sheila's Blog *The Life of a Retired Teacher*

Home   About   Blog   Photos   Archive

Class Reunion – 1 week to go

The class reunion is next week! I'm very excited about it, but I'm also nervous. I taught this class a long time ago, in 1986. I used to love them! They were really interesting students. Last week, I came across some of their old work, some of their old pictures and the stories they wrote. But there was also something else. In 1986, they all wrote down their ambitions in life. I've taken some photos of them and posted them here. I think they're lovely, and they really made me laugh. At the reunion I really want to hear about their lives, and what they've achieved. I especially want to meet Sue and John again. They always worked really hard, and John made me laugh. And Nabeel! He was always so shy and serious.

When I grow up, I want to be a princess. Sue

I'm going to be the president when I grow up. There will be no school. Nabeel

When I grow up, I'm going to eat lots of chocolate and explode! If I'm really strong, I'm going to be a firefighter. Nancy

When I grow up, I want everything. Maia

When I grow up, I'm going to be Batman. John

When I'm older, I'd like to stay at home and do nothing. But if I'm tall, I'm going to be a basketball player. Rosa

b 💬 Work in pairs and answer the question.

1 What do you think happened to John, Sue and Nabeel when they left school? What do you think they're doing now?

c Now read blog post 2, *Our Special Evening*. Were your guesses correct?

Blog post 2

| Home | About | Blog | Photos | Archive | |

Our Special Evening

So, we had the class reunion last night. It was so wonderful to see my former students again. You'll never believe what they're all doing now! It was really interesting to catch up with them.

John didn't become Batman, but he's had a really crazy life. He's been married three times and has eight kids! His sons now all want to be Batman, just like he did! He's working in two different jobs at the moment. He's a taxi driver and he also owns a small shop – a toy shop! What else? He told me he wants to pay for his kids to get a good education. He said he wants to become a teacher one day – he was only joking!

Sue has passed all her exams and got excellent grades at high school. She then got a degree in engineering and now she works for NASA. She isn't an astronaut, but she did work on a mission to the moon. She's amazing! It just shows: if you work hard, you'll succeed.

Nabeel didn't become the president or prime minister. He said he hates politics. He's a successful actor now. He does comedy on national radio! He is so funny.

d Read blog post 2 again. Answer the questions.

1 Who has changed a lot?
2 Who had a really good education?
3 Who does Sheila think has done well?

e Are the statements true or false? Correct the false statements. Compare your answers with a partner.

1 Nabeel used to be interested in politics.
2 Rosa wanted to be a firefighter when she was a child.
3 John has two jobs to pay for his education.
4 Sue has been on a mission to the moon.
5 Nabeel isn't shy and serious any more.

3 SPEAKING

a 💬 Work in groups. Discuss the questions together.

1 Have you ever been to a class reunion? What was it like? If you haven't, would you like to?
2 What do you think happened to your old classmates?
3 Who was the best teacher you had at school? Why? Who was the worst? Why?

1 SPEAKING

a 🗨 Read situations A and B below. Work in pairs. Which company do you think provides the best customer service? Why?

A Your luggage is lost during a flight. There's no one to help you. You have to go online to complain. There is no apology, but they find your luggage in five minutes.

B You ordered a book online but the website sent you the wrong one. You call the free customer services phone line. The person is friendly, polite and professional, and they apologise. But it takes two weeks to get the right book.

2 READING 1

a Read the extract from an article about customer service below. Are the statements true or false? Compare your ideas with a partner.

1 More than 50% of customers would pay extra if they knew they would have a good experience.

2 A lot of customers complain when they are not happy with a company's services or products.

3 It's easier for companies to get new customers than to keep their old customers happy.

4 55% of customers use social media to complain to customer services.

Good Customer Service?

Research by an organisation called *thinkJar* has found that 55% of customers would pay more money if they had a guarantee of a positive customer experience, but they are tired of promises. So, are people receiving good customer service?

There is an old saying that 'no news is good news' but it isn't always true, especially when it comes to customer service. When companies don't get much negative feedback, they often think it's a good thing. But in fact, it's the opposite. Research by thinkJar shows that only one out of every 26 customers complains when they're not happy. Over 90% of unhappy customers say nothing and just change to a different company. This is a serious problem for businesses because it is much more difficult to attract new customers than to keep existing ones. Have you ever asked yourself why, for example, many phone companies and banks offer better conditions to new customers?

Communicating with customer services should be easier than in the past. But is it? There are more ways than ever for customers to give feedback – by phone, letter, email or live chats. Social media is a popular way for people to complain or ask for information, but many companies are not using social media in the most effective way. In fact, studies show that 55% of customers' requests on social media are never answered!

3 VOCABULARY

Match the words (1–6) with definitions (a–f). Compare your answers with a partner.

1 ☐ sort out (an issue)   4 ☐ nightmare
2 ☐ dough   5 ☐ concern
3 ☐ upside-down   6 ☐ on the house

a a horrible experience
b a worried or nervous feeling
c deal well with a situation or problem
d turned so that the top part is at the bottom
e free of charge
f flour and water mixed to cook bread

4 READING 2

a Read the complaints to customer services below. Answer the questions.

1 Which situation do you think is the most serious? Which is the funniest?
2 Who do you think provides the best customer service? Why?

b 💬 Compare your answers in pairs.

BETTER READING:
UNDERSTANDING PRONOUN REFERENCE

To understand the links across a text, created by pronouns, it is important to understand what the pronouns refer to.

1 What does each use of *it* refer to in conversation 3? Match 1–7 to A, B, C or D.

A the issue	C taking the photo
B the photo	D the necklace

c Read the complaints in 4a again and answer the questions.

1 Why is @PatrickT eating alone?
2 What two problems has Adam had with pizzas?
3 How did @Yellnow sort out the problem?
4 Why is @SusanR worried about being late for her friend?
5 What does @Edenman think will happen if the café queues continue in future?

5 SPEAKING

a Think about the best and worst customer service you've ever received. Where was it? When?

b 💬 Work in groups of three or four. Tell each other your stories. Which person has had the best service? Who's had the worst?

Complaints | These days, customer services departments deal with complaints and much more! Read our top complaints!

1 More sauce, please!

I've just been served a steak in one of your restaurants, and there isn't enough sauce. Where are all your staff?

Hi @PatrickT, sorry about that. Could you tell us which restaurant you are in?

I'd rather not. My wife thinks I'm at work.

Okay @PatrickT! We just hope she doesn't read your tweets!

Oh! Yes, thanks for the warning! I've had a long day at work and just needed to have a nice quiet meal. Anyway, I'm just going to delete these.

OK, @PatrickT. Did you manage to sort out the problem with the sauce?

Yes, but please stop tweeting me! My wife will wonder why.

2 Pizza problems

I ordered a pizza, but there's nothing on it, no cheese or anything. It's just a piece of pizza dough! Last week, I had a pizza and there wasn't enough cheese, but this is worse!

Hi @AdamW. We're sorry about this. Please let @NYPizza know so they can help you.

Never mind! I opened the pizza box upside-down.

3 Trouble at the gym

I'm having a bit of an issue with something in your gym, and I was wondering if you could help.

Thanks for letting us know @Yellnow. Could you tell us a little bit more about [1]it?

Well, maybe I could take a photo and send [2]it to you?

Yes, please. That would really help.

No, I can't do [3]it. I can't get my phone in the right place. Hold on. I'll ask someone to take [4]it for me. No, he couldn't do [5]it either. Okay [6]it's all sorted now.

That's great news! What was the problem?

I had my necklace stuck in the exercise machine. I was pulling on [7]it, but it was stuck! What a nightmare! No jewellery next time!

4 Bookshop blues

Hello @DBS! I've just been locked inside your bookshop! I shouted but the security guy was too far away. Can anyone help?! I've got to meet a friend in 25 minutes!

Hello again @DBS. Just to say I can't tweet long. I don't have enough battery. My friend's never going to believe me if I'm late! I've been late twice before already!

We're sending someone right away @SusanR. Give us fifteen minutes. We'll have you out in time! We would never want our bookshop to get in the way of friends!

We are happy to announce that @SusanR is a free woman! Thank you for everyone's concern and tweets! We hope she has a lovely evening!

5 Tired of waiting

I'm at your café on Denmark Street, and there are too many people. The queue goes all the way to the end of the street!

We apologise for this, @Edenman. We are clearly too popular!

Not for much longer if you have queues like this! You need to do something about it!

@Edenman, we understand your concern and we are sorry for the delay today. Please show this tweet to your barista to claim a coffee on the house.

1 SPEAKING

a 💬 Work in pairs. How many hours a day do you spend … ?

1 awake
2 using technology or online
3 watching video (e.g. on phones, tablets, TV)
4 listening to the radio
5 communicating via social media, emailing or texting

b 💬 Compare your answers with the rest of the class. Who uses technology the most?

2 READING 1

a Read *Technology Half Life* below. Answer the questions.

1 On average, how much time do people spend doing the activities described in 1a.
2 According to the article, what's the advantage of using technology so much?
3 Work in groups. Do you use technology more or less than the average? Are you surprised by the research? Why / Why not?

Technology Half Life

We now spend half of our lives using technology, according to a recent survey. Most people's days are 15 hours 45 minutes long, and for 45% of that time we are online or using some kind of technology.

Adults spend on average 212 minutes a day watching video (e.g. on phones, tablets, TV), 91 minutes a day listening to the radio, and 80 minutes a day text messaging, on social media or emailing.

We also now tend to do more than one thing at once. We check social media while we watch TV, or we send an email while we're cooking. One of the positive things about all this technology is that we are getting better at multitasking.

 BETTER READING: ORGANISATION OF IDEAS

It helps you understand if you see how a text is organised. Sometimes, newspaper articles are organised like this:

general idea > more details > comment

Look at the newspaper article in 2a again.
1 underline the general idea <u>like this</u>.
2 underline more details <u>like this</u>.
3 underline the comment <u>like this</u>.

3 READING 2

a 💬 You are going to read about the website challenge *48 Hours without Technology* on page 59. Which people do you think would find it most difficult to live without technology? Why?

children   teenagers   people in their 20s and 30s people over 40   people over 70

b Read Julia's diary on page 59. Was her life without technology …?

1 positive   2 negative   3 both positive and negative

c Read Julia's diary again. Answer the questions.

1 Which piece of technology does Julia think she will miss the most? Why?
2 Why does Julia go to the shop?
3 What three things does Julia do, which she says she she's never done?
4 What four things does she talk to her dad about?
5 Why did Julia sleep well?
6 Why didn't Julia's friends talk to her at lunchtime?

4 SPEAKING

a 💬 Discuss the questions together.

1 Would you like to spend 48 hours without technology? Why / Why not?
2 What would you do if you didn't have technology for 48 hours?
3 Do you think we depend on technology too much? Why / Why not?
4 Do you think phones and tablets should be banned in these situations?
   • during lessons
   • on public transport
   • during lunchtime at work
   • your own ideas

b 💬 Imagine there was no technology in other areas of life. What would be the advantages and disadvantages?
   • schools
   • universities
   • the workplace
   • the home

48 Hours without Technology

In our new series, we've asked five people of different ages to spend 48 hours without any phones, tablets or laptops, and to tell us about their experiences. This week it was Julia's turn. Did she survive?

Julia is a 25-year-old office manager. She lives at home in Melbourne, Australia, with her parents.

Day 1

7.00
Just woken up. I'm really nervous about this challenge. I'm most worried about my phone. It's a part of me really, like an arm or a leg. And I watch a lot of TV, too.

7.10
I am so bored! I keep wondering what my friends are doing, but I suppose I'll see them at work.

7.15
My parents are still in bed, and I've still got over an hour before I leave for work. I think I'll go to the shop.

7.45
That was really strange! I think that's the first time I've walked down the street without my phone. I didn't like it – it felt strange. Ended up buying my first newspaper!

8.30
Had to have a nightmare conversation with my dad at breakfast. I love him, but I don't like having a conversation about my life in the morning! He said every time I'm bored I should read an article in the newspaper.

10.30
My neighbour was at the bus stop. She said her name's Agnes and she gets the same bus every morning. I've never had a conversation with her before. She's lovely!

22.00
That was the worst and best evening! I was so bored and felt really frustrated! Then I read some fascinating articles in the newspaper, which I bought this morning, and I ended up having this really interesting chat with my dad about his school days and work. He gave me some great advice. It's made me think that I might change jobs.

Day 2

7.00
I had the best night's sleep of my life! My phone always wakes me up with notifications, and I always check it. But last night it was very quiet. I feel great this morning!

12.00
I've just had an argument with one of my colleagues. She was very rude to me. I feel really upset. I really want to post something about it on Facebook, but I can't! That's the problem with not having my phone. I can't immediately share what's happened to me with my friends. That's the worst thing about not having a phone. I miss my friends. When I have my phone, I feel like they are always with me.

14.30
Lunchtime was quite boring. We all went to the café as usual, and they were all checking their phones. We were all sitting together, but no one was talking. They were all in their own private worlds.

There was a mum and her little girl at the next table. The mum was on her phone. I had a little chat with the girl. She said, 'My mum says I can't have a phone. You don't have a phone. Is that because your mummy said you can't have one?'

Day 3

7.00
Well, I have my phone back! It's been a really interesting 48 hours. I feel like so many cool things have happened. I got to know my dad and my neighbour better. I read more than I have for ages. I slept really well. But I did really miss communicating with my friends.

So, I've decided I'm going to only use my phone during the evening now, not in the day. We'll see how that will change my life!

1 SPEAKING

a 💬 Work in pairs. Do you think the sentences below are true or false?

1 There are about 500 million twins in the world.
2 Twins always have the same appearance and the same personality.
3 Twins sometimes grow up in different places, but have the same lives (e.g. job, free-time activities).
4 People do research into twins to understand personality better.
5 There is a twins' festival every year in the USA.

2 READING

a Read the magazine article on page 61 about twins. Were your answers to 1a correct?

b Look at the article again. Find the highlighted adjectives in the text and match them to definitions 1–7 below.

1 quiet, not comfortable being with other people _____
2 a relaxed person, who doesn't get annoyed easily

_____
3 when you know someone well and like them _____
4 someone who enjoys meeting other people _____
5 usually nervous and worried _____
6 looking exactly the same _____
7 a quiet person who doesn't laugh very much _____

> **BETTER READING:**
> **UNDERSTANDING PARAGRAPH STRUCTURE**
>
> It can help you to understand a text better if you understand the organisation of a paragraph. Sometimes, paragraphs are organised like this: the general idea > more detailed information
>
> **1** Look at paragraph 5 in the article.
>   a Underline the general idea <u>like this</u>.
>   b Underline more information <u>like this</u>.

c Read the article again more carefully. Which twins do sentences 1–6 refer to? Write *C* (for Chris and Julian), *A* (for Ahmed and Mohammed), *M* (for Melissa and Joyce) *F* (for Fred and Jack), or *J* (for Jim and Jim).

1 They have different talents.
2 People thought they were one person.
3 They lived in different places when they were young. (x2)
4 They do the same romantic thing for their wives.
5 They like exactly the same food.
6 No one can understand when they speak to each other.

3 SPEAKING

a 💬 Ask and answer the questions with a partner.

1 Do you know any twins? Do they look identical? Do they have similar personalities?
2 Would you like to have a twin? Why / Why not?
3 Do you know anyone who looks similar to their brother or sister? Do you know any siblings who have very similar personalities?
4 Do you think the environment or genes is a bigger influence on personality? Talk about people you know.

Twice as Amazing

Welcome to the amazing world of twins. There are about 250 million in the world. Some do maths tests for each other, and others even marry people with the same names. We went to the Twins Day Festival in Twinsburg, Ohio, to find out more about some of their lives.

Fred and Jack have come to the festival for years. They look the same. They both have long red beards. But they are different in other ways. Fred is good at maths, and Jack has always been a good cook. Their parents wanted them to be individuals, so they went to different schools.

Fred said people had always confused them. One day, Jack had a maths test, and he sent his brother instead. 'He got an A!' Jack said. About ten years ago, Fred prepared the food at a big private party. He asked his brother to help, and asked him to wear the same clothes. The guests were amazed! Fred said everyone believed he was doing the job of two men!

They spend every day together. 'We're very close,' Fred said. 'We're both quite easy-going and sociable, though Jack is more serious than I am. We had a week apart last year. I had to stay in hospital. Afterwards, Jack said it had been the longest week of his life.'

There are identical twins who grew up apart, but met later in life. Joyce grew up in Florida, but her sister Melissa grew up in California. They never knew about each other. But they both became nurses and were artists in their free time. And they were both always very anxious and shy people. When they met at the age of 50, Joyce told Melissa she'd always known she had a twin sister.

The most famous example of identical twins is probably the Jim twins. They were adopted by different parents at birth, and brought up hundreds of kilometres apart. 39 years later, they met each other for the first time, and discovered they had a lot in common.

Both men were six feet tall and weighed 180 pounds. As young men, they'd both married women named Linda, and then divorced them. Their second wives were both named Betty. They named their sons James Alan and James Allan. And they both left love notes around the house for their wives.

Scientists are doing a lot of research at the festival. In one tent, twins Ahmed and Mohammed have just finished trying different dishes from around the world. Researcher John Halifax says, 'they appear to have the same taste.' He believes twins can answer a lot of questions. 'We are doing research into the biggest [question] of all – about personality. What is more important, genes or the environment, nature or nurture?'

Halifax said twins would always surprise us. 'I met two brothers, Chris and Julian, this morning who have their own language. They seem to have their own special vocabulary and grammar. They're amazing.'

The publishers would like to thank the authors, Adrian Doff, Craig Thaine and David Rea for their work on these academic skills and reading lessons.

The authors and publishers acknowledge the following sources of copyright material and are grateful for the permissions granted. While every effort has been made, it has not always been possible to identify the sources of all the material used, or to trace all copyright holders. If any omissions are brought to our notice, we will be happy to include the appropriate acknowledgements on reprinting and in the next update to the digital edition, as applicable.

Key: T = Top, B = Below, TL = Top Left, BR = Bottom Right, CL = Centre Left, TR = Top Right, L= Left, R= Right, U = Unit.

Academic Skills

Text Acknowledgements

U5 p. 18: Independent Digital News & Media Ltd for the text adapted from 'The Realities of Balancing Employment with your Studies' by Natasha Preskey, *The Independent*, 11.02.2014. Copyright © 2014 Independent Digital News & Media Ltd. Reproduced with permission; U7 p. 24: Telegraph Group Media Limited for the text adapted from 'How young is too young for technology?' by Josie Gurney-Read, *The Telegraph*, 02.12.2013. Copyright © 2013 Telegraph Group Media Limited. Reproduced with permission; U10 p. 31: Ascential Group Limited for the text adapted from 'Analysis: Automation and the future of the retail workforce' by Susie Mesure, RetailWeek website, 04.05.2016. Copyright © 2016 Ascential Group Limited. Reproduced with kind permission; U12 p. 37: PsychCentral.com for the text adapted from 'Leaving Home Sooner or Later: What Does It Mean for Your Relationship with Your Parents down the Road?' by Bella DePaulo. Copyright © 2017 PsychCentral.com. All rights reserved. Reprinted here with kind permission.

Photo Acknowledgements

All the photographs are sourced from Getty Images.

U1 p. 6 (a): Christian Science Monitor; U1 p. 6 (b): Dave and Les Jacobs/Blend Images; U1 p. 6 (c): monkeybusinessimages/iStock/Getty Images Plus; U1 p. 6 (d): Vincent Besnault/Photographer's Choice; U2 p. 8 (a): Marco Di Lauro/Getty Images News; U2 p. 8 (b): John Harper/The Image Bank; U2 p. 9: DmitryLityagin/iStock/ Getty Images Plus; U2 p. 11: Image Source/DigitalVision; U3 p. 12 (L): Hoxton/Tom Merton; U3 p. 12 (R): Sloniki/iStock/Getty Images Plus; U3 p. 13: Graiki/Moment; U4 p. 14 (L): verity jane smith/Blend Images; U4 p. 14 (R): Mixmike/E+; U4 p. 15: Tara Moore/Taxi; U5 p. 16: Westend61; U5 p. 18: Jochen Sand/Photodisc; U6 p. 19 (spiders): TorriPhoto/Moment; U6 p. 19 (flying): 172285838/E+; U6 p. 19 (height): SimonDannhauer/iStock/Getty Images Plus; U6 p. 19 (train): Alex Segre/Moment Mobile; U7 p. 21: Ute Grabowsky/Photothek; U7 p. 22: Cultura RM Exclusive/Igor Emmerich; U7 p. 24: Adrian Weinbrecht/Collection; U8 p. 25 (woman): Tetra Images; U8 p. 25 (man): Oliver Rossi/Corbis; U8 p. 26: Tim Robberts/The Image Bank; U9 p. 27 (L): Troy Aossey/Taxi; U9 p. 27 (R): Peter Cade/The Image Bank; U9 p. 28: martin-dm/E+; U10 p. 29 (a): UpperCut Images; U10 p. 29 (b): John Greim/ LightRocket; U10 p. 29 (c): Joos Mind/The Image Bank; U10 p. 30: sturti/E+; U10 p. 31: THEGIFT777/iStock/Getty Images Plus; U11 p. 32 (TR): Kathrin Ziegler/Taxi; U11 p. 32 (CL): Marc O. Finley/StockFood Creative; U11 p. 32 (BR): Kryssia Campos/ Moment; U11 p. 33: Ivenks/iStock/Getty Images Plus; U12 p. 34 (TL): MartinPrescott/ E+; U12 p. 34 (TR): Fredrik Telleus/Maskot; U12 p. 34 (B): laflor/iStock/Getty Images Plus; U12 p. 35: Kim Kirby/LOOP IMAGES/Corbis Documentary; U12 p. 36: William King/The Image Bank; U12 p. 37: Kevin Dodge/Blend Images.

Audio production by Hart McLeod, Cambridge.

Reading Plus

Photo Acknowledgements

All the photographs are sourced from Getty Images.

U1 p. 38 (T): Sam Edwards/OJO Images; U1 p. 38 (a): Adrianko/Cultura; U1 p. 38 (b): Glowimages; U1 p. 38 (c): JGI/Tom Grill/Blend Images; U1 p. 38 (d): Johner Images; U1 p. 38 (e), U5 p. 47 (B), U7 p. 50: Westend61; U1 p. 38 (f): AAGAMIA/The Image Bank; U2 p. 40 (L): thomasandreas/iStock/Getty Images Plus; U2 p. 40 (R): Take A Pix Media/ Blend Images; U3 p. 43 (T): Universal Images Group; U3 p. 43 (B): Olaf Herschbach/ EyeEm; U4 p. 44: Doug Armand/Photolibrary; U4 p. 45 (T): CHRIS RATCLIFFE/Stringer/ AFP; U4 p. 45 (B): mikeinlondon/iStock Editorial/Getty Images Plus; U5 p. 47 (T): Tempura/E+; U6 p. 48 (a): KAZUHIRO NOGI/AFP; U6 p. 48 (b): Multi-bits/The Image Bank; U6 p. 48 (c): Joe McBride/Stone; U6 p. 48 (d): Galen Rowell/Corbis Documentary; U6 p. 48 (e): kadmy/iStock/Getty Images Plus; U6 p. 49: Bernhard Limberger/LOOKfoto; U8 p. 52: andresr/E+; U8 p. 53: petrzurek/iStock/Getty Images Plus; U9 p. 54: Elyse Lewin/Photographer's Choice; U9 p. 55: Emir Memedovski/E+; U10 p. 56 (T): Brad Wilson/The Image Bank; U10 p. 56 (B), U11 p. 59: Yuri_Arcurs/DigitalVision; U12 p. 60 (T): AND-ONE/iStock/Getty Images Plus; U12 p. 60 (B): Vasilina Popova/DigitalVision; U12 p. 61: Barcroft Media.